BATTER UP!
AMAZING BASEBALL TRIVIA

Edited by Ross Berger

STERLING INNOVATION
An imprint of Sterling Publishing Co., Inc.

New York / London
www.sterlingpublishing.com

STERLING, the Sterling logo, STERLING INNOVATION, and the Sterling Innovation logo are registered trademarks of Sterling Publishing Co., Inc.

Library of Congress Cataloging-in-Publication Data

Batter up! : amazing baseball trivia / edited by Ross Berger.
   p. cm.
  Includes index.
  ISBN 978-1-4027-6725-8
  1. Baseball--United States--Miscellanea. I. Berger, Ross.
  GV873.B32 2009
  796.357--dc22

                    2008054411

10 9 8 7 6 5 4 3 2 1

Published by Sterling Publishing Co., Inc.
387 Park Avenue South, New York, NY 10016
© 2009 by Sterling Publishing Co., Inc.

This book is comprised of materials from the following
Sterling Publishing Co., Inc. titles:
Match Wits with Baseball Experts © 2006 by Wayne Stewart
All-New Baseball Brainteasers © 2006 by Michael A. Morse
The Little Giant Encyclopedia of Baseball Quizzes © 2005 by
The Idea Logical Company

Distributed in Canada by Sterling Publishing
c/o Canadian Manda Group, 165 Dufferin Street
Toronto, Ontario, Canada M6K 3H6
Distributed in the United Kingdom by GMC Distribution Services
Castle Place, 166 High Street, Lewes, East Sussex, England BN7 1XU
Distributed in Australia by Capricorn Link (Australia) Pty. Ltd.
P.O. Box 704, Windsor, NSW 2756, Australia

Design by StarGraphics Studio

Sterling ISBN 978-1-4027-6725-8

For information about custom editions, special sales, premium and
corporate purchases, please contact Sterling Special Sales
Department at 800-805-5489 or specialsales@sterlingpublishing.com.

CONTENTS

INTRODUCTION

IN THIS BOOK YOU WILL BE ASKED to put yourself into the spiked cleats of baseball players, the shoes of managers and umpires in the field, and the suits of those manning the teams' front offices. You'll compete against real members of Major League teams, testing your knowledge against theirs.

Your decisions can sway the outcome of historical big league games when you step into the place of legendary managers Walter Alston and Connie Mack. Take on today's challenges with puzzlers faced by contemporary skippers such as Joe Torre, Dusty Baker, and Mike Hargrove. You can choose to play the percentages, as many managers do, or take an occasional risk and go against the "book." You may decide to call for a triple steal or even a suicide squeeze play. You may decide to yank a pitcher or let him tough it out despite a rising pitch count.

You'll be asked what call to make when you're the "man in black" and a play gets complicated. Was that a foul tip or was the pitch tipped foul? What's the difference? Baseball is one of America's best-loved sports, but what fans and even players think of as "common knowledge" is often just plain wrong. There is confusion and even ignorance about the basic rules and terms of the game. Do you know enough to sort it all out and make the right call when a big game is on the line? Don't forget, a little common sense can go a long way toward understanding the correct call.

In addition to your role-playing tasks, at times not only will your knowledge of baseball rules and strategy be put to the test, but your general baseball I.Q. dealing with records, trivia, and even quotes will also be under fire.

HOW TO USE THIS BOOK

THIS BOOK CAN BE READ from front to back or taken one quiz at a time in any order. The questions appear in the front of the chapter and the answers are in the back. You will find many types of questions. One might describe a situation, and you have to figure out what the ruling was, what strategy should be used, or which ballplayer is being portrayed. Often you will find not only the answer in the back of the chapter, but also what game the question was taken from and a detailed description of the correct call on the play.

Other questions are a simple matter of multiple-choice. These questions often deal with stats, records, years, and player trivia. The answers may be more matter-of-fact than making a tough call on a wild play, but that doesn't mean they'll be easier to answer!

In this book your fandom will be tested from every angle as you prove your knowledge of the rules, strategies, facts, stats, and history of the game. You have your work cut out for you, so read on and take the challenge!

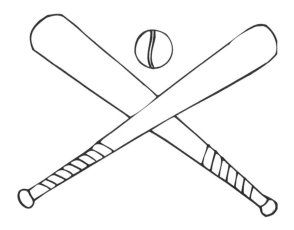

Chapter 1

Batting

CAN YOU NAME THESE WORLD-CLASS BATTERS?

Test your knowledge of star players by reading clues and identifying the "speakers," and by answering questions on hits, plays, and stats.

1. HIT 'EM WHERE THEY ARE

My strike zone is as big as my eyes. That is to say, I like to swing at virtually any pitch, anywhere—I've been known to hoist pitches from down near the top of my spikes for homers and I've been known to tee off on pitches up to my eyes. The results are the same: awesome. I won an MVP Award in the American League and I've hit for power and average every season since my real season in the Bigs, not counting 1996 when I was up for a brief "sip of coffee." In fact, the .302 I hit in 1997 is the lowest I've hit in the majors. As for my power numbers, from 1998 to 2006, I've hit 30 or more homers eight times, the same amount of times I've driven home 100 or more runs. Who am I?

The answer is on page 30.

2. THEY CALL ME "PAPI"

My nickname alone might give my identity away. I am a dead pull hitter who amasses homers the way Disney's Scrooge McDuck piled up moolah. What a treat it was to be a part (a big part, with 41 homers and 139 RBI) of the 2004 world champion Boston Red Sox. Three years later, my .332 average helped the Bosox win yet another World Series championship. All this was after finding my first big league success with the Minnesota Twins as a first sacker and a designated hitter. Can you ID me?

The answer is on page 30.

3. I CAN DO IT ALL

I have won Gold Glove awards but am more famous for my bat. In 2005, I became only the fourth man ever to hit 500 or more homers while also owning 3,000 or more hits. I did so while in the Baltimore Orioles jersey. Who am I?

The answer is on page 30.

4. WHAT A COINCIDENCE!

I am a .303 lifetime hitter, but I also have the distinction of making the final out in two no-hitters authored by the same pitcher, doing so in 1963 and 1965. I guided the Milwaukee Brewers to a World Series appearance in 1982, losing in seven games to the Cardinals. Who am I?

The answer is on page 30.

5. HE'S A SLAMMER

I began my big league career with the Texas Rangers, whose co-managing general partner was George W. Bush. In an ill-fated trade, I was sent to the White Sox. My most recent team has been the Orioles. This next clue should give my identity away: From 1998 through 2001 I averaged almost exactly 61 homers per season with blistering totals of 66, 63, 50, and 64 round-trippers. Who am I?

The answer is on page 30.

6. GIVE 'EM THE THUMB, TWICE!

Odd one: In 1946, having retired as a member of the 500 home run club, I became the first manager to be ejected from both ends of a doubleheader. That day my New York Giants were swept by the Pittsburgh Pirates. Who am I?

The answer is on page 30.

7. 3,000 HITS AND COUNTING

On June 9, 1914, I became the first man ever to reach the 3,000 hits plateau and I went on to stroke an additional 430 before I hung up my cleats. Who am I?

The answer is on page 30.

8. HOME RUNS GALORE

Many of my myriad home runs did not fly majestically out of parks, but rather followed a line drive trajectory as they cleared the walls. They still tell the story of the time I lifted a line drive over the shortstop who leaped to try to snag the ball; seconds later, the ball, still rising, left the park. My bat was said to be quicker than a University of Miami defensive back. I hold countless records, including the most runs driven in over a career, 2,297, which works out to an average of 99.9 RBI for each of my 23 seasons in the majors. Who am I?

The answer is on page 30.

9. ANOTHER HOME RUN KING

When I came to the plate, third basemen tended to position themselves very deep, almost as if they were softball rovers in the outfield. No wonder. I pulled the ball as hard as a Dick Butkus forearm smash. One longtime fan observed, "All you have to do to know who the wicked pull hitters are is look at where the third base coach stands when a guy's up and there's no traffic to direct." When I hit, my third base coach always distanced himself from me and the really hot corner; at times, it seemed like he wished he was a bullpen coach, rather than a base coach.

My biggest accomplishment came when I was with the Cardinals, but I had been a Rookie of the Year with the Oakland

A's in 1987, setting home run records early on. I wound up with 583 lifetime homers. Who am I?

The answer is on page 30.

10. PHILLY SLUGGER

Lee Smith made this observation about me: "He had some of the quickest and strongest hands as I've ever seen on a hitter. He was unbelievable. You could make good pitches and he'd just golf balls right off the ground." I was with the Phillies for my entire 18-year career. I retired in 1989 as an eight-time home run king and with nearly 1,600 runs driven in. Who am I?

The answer is on page 31.

11. GLOWING WORDS

My one-time Angels teammate Doug DeCinces commented, "The difference between this guy and the rest of us is that when we get hot, we go up to .300. When he gets hot, he goes up to .500." Former infielder Alan Bannister was cited in Baseball Quotations as joking, "He's the only guy I know who can go four-for-three." Finally, pitcher Ken Holtzman observed, "He has an uncanny ability to move the ball around as if the bat were some kind of magic wand." I was always aware of where the defense played me and did what it took to get on base—be it lay down a bunt or lash out a line drive. I wound up with 3,053 lifetime hits. Who am I?

The answer is on page 31.

12. CAN'T WHIFF HIM

A Hall of Fame outfielder, I was extremely difficult to strike out. Over my illustrious career, spent entirely as a New York Yankee, I struck out just 369 times. I also hit .325 lifetime with 361 home runs. Usually batters with some clout will fan frequently—it's an occupational hazard. In my case, though, things were quite different. My ratio of almost exactly one home run for every strikeout is the lowest in the history of the game for men with 300 or more homers. Who am I?

The answer is on page 31.

13. CAN'T WHIFF HIM, PART II

I am second, trailing only a teammate of mine, for the best career ratio of homers-to-strikeouts as I hit 358 homers and went down on strikes only 415 times. My lifetime average was .285, and my other achievements, including those as a manager, earned a spot for me in the Hall of Fame as well. I had a reputation for hacking away at pitches almost regardless of their locations, but I got the job done. I even took home three MVP Awards and was named to 15 All-Star contests. Who am I?

The answer is on page 31.

14. TAG TEAM

Two men from the same team seldom wind up one-two for the RBI leadership in a league, and it's even more rare for teammates to tie for the lead. In 1928, for instance, Lou Gehrig and Babe Ruth shared the lead with 142 runs driven in each. The next time that feat occurred was in 1949, when two Red Sox players drove in a whopping 159 runs apiece. I did this, and the teammate who matched me was Vern Stephens.

Additionally, I am one of only two men to win the Triple Crown on two occasions. Ironically, I didn't win the MVP in either of my Triple Crown seasons, but I did win that trophy twice. Who am I?

The answer is on page 31.

◆ ◆ ◆

NOW IT'S TIME FOR SOME TRIVIA!

15. CHRISTENING YANKEE STADIUM

The first game ever played at Yankee Stadium took place on April 18, 1923. Who hit the first homer ever at that venue?

The answer is on page 31.

16. LET THERE BE A DH

The first use of a designated hitter took place on an Opening Day when a Yankee stepped into the box and drew a walk. Name that man or, within three years, guess when this occurred.

The answer is on page 31.

17. HISTORY IS MADE

The Atlanta versus Cincinnati lid-lifter of April 4, 1974, featured an historic event. Jack Billingham delivered a pitch that a member of the Braves pulled crisply for a monumental record-tying homer. Who was the batter and what was the significance of the home run?

The answer is on page 31.

18. A FIRST "FIRST"

Nicknamed "Dewey," this man also made history, doing so on April 7, 1986, when he smacked the very first pitch of the new season for a round tripper, connecting for the Red Sox against Jack Morris and the Tigers. Clue: his initials are D.E.

The answer is on page 32.

19. HE LOVES OPENERS

What man hit more home runs on Opening Day than any other man? Clue: His most famous homer in an Opener came when he was a player-manager for the Indians in 1975.

The answer is on page 32.

20. A Final "First"

Who was the first player ever to hit 30 or more homers in a season; the first to reach 40-plus homers; and the first to attain the 50-home-run plateau?

The answer is on page 32.

21. CAREER BEGINNINGS

Can you match the sluggers with the team these sluggers broke in with?

1. Babe Ruth	A. Milwaukee Braves
2. Hank Aaron	B. Pittsburgh Pirates
3. Barry Bonds	C. Boston Red Sox
4. Willie Mays	D. Cincinnati Reds
5. Frank Robinson	E. New York Giants

The answer is on page 32.

22. MORE CAREER BEGINNINGS

Match these .300-caliber hitters to the teams with which they began their Major League careers:

1. Larry Walker	A. Seattle Mariners
2. Sean Casey	B. Chicago Cubs
3. Rod Carew	C. Cleveland Indians
4. Rafael Palmeiro	D. Montreal Expos
5. Alex Rodriguez	E. Minnesota Twins

The answer is on page 32.

23. FINAL DAY DRAMATICS

The 1950 regular season had a dramatic conclusion in the National League. The Phillies and Dodgers had raged through a hard-fought pennant race that came down to the last game of the year, which just happened to be between these two pennant-hungry clubs. Even then, at the end of nine innings they were deadlocked at one run apiece. Finally, in the tenth inning, a Philadelphia outfielder took Don Newcombe deep to win it all as the Phillies earned their first trip to the World Series since 1915. Tough one: Who hit the game-winning homer? His initials are D.S., and his father, George, was a Hall of Famer who had twice hit .400, topping out at a sparkling .420 in 1922.

The answer is on page 32.

24. FAMOUS FINISH

One of the most memorable events from a final game came in 1941 when Ted Williams, perched comfortably on a .400-plus average, refused to sit out a season-ending doubleheader. He not only played both ends, he banged out six hits to elevate his batting average to a heady .406 mark. Who was his manager who offered to let Williams rest on the pines? Clues: He is a Hall of Famer, a great Red Sox hitter himself, with the initials J.C.

The answer is on page 32.

25. STRANGE BATTING CROWN BATTLE

As the 1910 season wound down, Nap Lajoie and his Cleveland Naps (nicknamed in honor of Lajoie). played St. Louis in a doubleheader on October 9. The popular Lajoie trailed a despised player for the league lead in batting by a wide spread. Lajoie needed an eight-for-nine showing to snare the batting title.

Thanks to some help from a cooperative Browns defense, that is exactly what he got.

St. Louis manager Jack O'Connor instructed his rookie third baseman to play deep, way out by the outfield grass, a defensive deployment that came into play by Lajoie's third at bat. His first two times to the plate produced a clean triple and a bunt single on a ball fielded by shortstop Bobby Wallace. Things changed, though, over his next seven trips to the plate as Lajoie placed bunts down the third base line—six resulted in hits.

Lajoie had, it appeared, won the batting crown. However, the American League, embarrassed by St. Louis' shenanigans, eventually took action. On October 15, league president Ban Johnson announced that, after final calculations had been made, Lajoie had actually lost the title by a microscopic gap of .384944 to the other star's .384084. What player was awarded the batting crown?

The answer is on page 32.

26. A REALLY LONG BALL

Fred McGriff has hit more than his share of homers and witnessed even more. Looking back through all the titanic blasts he's seen, the home run he felt was the most stupendous ever was one that was jacked completely out of Milwaukee County Stadium. "I thought that was incredible because that's a huge stadium," catcher Rick Dempsey recalled. "Dan Plesac threw a fastball and it just disappeared into the night." He was correct—it sailed some thirty feet above an eight-foot-high fence above the left-field seats and was the only fair ball to escape that park. Who hit it, and, within three years, when was this feat performed? Clues: The player was an enormously strong member of the Detroit Tigers who also played with Toronto, where he fizzled; Japan, where he blossomed enough to result in his return to the United States; and, later in his career, he also played for the Yankees, Angels, and Indians. Additionally, he once swatted 51 homers and is the father of a talented baseball player named Prince.

The answer is on page 33.

27. FAMOUS RECORD
Start with two easy ones dealing with legendary records. This all-time great never hit more than 12 home runs in a given month nor more than 47 in a season, yet his name is synonymous with power.

The answer is on page 33.

28. ANOTHER FAMOUS RECORD
For sluggers, the 500 home run club is an exclusive group; to hit that many has been the equivalent of getting a free pass to the Hall of Fame. When it comes to pitchers, the 300 victory plateau is just as exclusive and magical. Name the only man with more than 500 wins.

The answer is on page 33.

29. A WHOLE LOT OF PRODUCTION
Ozzie Smith said the most impressive record that he witnessed was the "fascinating occurrence" when a St. Louis teammate hit a record-tying four home runs in a single game. Those homers also helped the player tie the record for the most runs driven in during a contest. Smith said that if his memory was correct, the player also walloped "the ball in the upper deck in Pittsburgh [Three River Stadium] all within a space of one week." Who is the man, and how many RBI did he collect during his spree?

The answer is on page 33.

30. MORE PRODUCTIVITY

Dave Winfield was with the Yankees when a teammate of his went berserk with the bat, setting a single season record for grand slams. Winfield remembered the player hitting "six grand slams in one year, all right in front of me, so I had a front row seat. He really cleared the bases; he had 24 RBI on six at bats!" Name the Yankee with the blistering bat.

The answer is on page 34.

31. BASEBALL'S METHUSELAH

Like Old Man River, this hitter just kept on churning and rolling along before his retirement in 2007. He turned 47 in August 2005, not long after he became the oldest player ever to steal a base. He also is the oldest ever to swat a pinch-hit homer, to play in 100 or more games, and to crush a grand slam. He journeyed and played around the globe, appearing in 42 big league parks as well as stadiums in Japan, South Korea, Mexico, Puerto Rico, and the Dominican Republic. Who is this ageless wonder?

The answer is on page 34.

32. HIT 'EM WHERE THEY AIN'T

His 242 hits as a rookie in 2001 were more than anyone had amassed in 71 years. Then, in 2004, his 262 hits (good for a lofty .372 average) shattered the ancient mark for the most hits in a single season. Opposing managers simply hope he swats the ball right at somebody, or puts it high enough in the air that the outfield can run it down.

Rickey Henderson critiqued this man's style, noting, "[He] can use a turf field to his advantage, he uses more of a running-type start, a swing-type start, to get him [going] and then he places the ball. To me, he's sort of like a Tony Gwynn guy who can put the ball anywhere they want to; and they basically try to put the ball in the holes." Henderson drew another comparison: "He is a little faster than [Rod] Carew. Carew was more of the scientist as a hitter. He hits the ball wherever it's pitched."

Who is this outstanding record holder?

The answer is on page 34.

33. FIRST TO TOP RUTH

Lately every baseball fan is well aware that the 60 home run mark is not quite as mystical as it once was. Who was the first man to surpass Babe Ruth's single season record of 60 homers in 1927?

The answer is on page 34.

34. TOP BATTING AVERAGE

The last man to reach the .400 strata was Ted Williams when he laced the ball to a .406 tune in 1941. Impressive to be sure, but the highest average for a single season was a mind-boggling .424. What superstar was able to hit that high?

The answer is on page 34.

35. TAKING A HIT

This man held numerous records for being hit by pitches. He'd often intentionally allow himself to get hit, at times resembling a walking bruise. He went so far as to purposely wear his uniform as baggy as possible, realizing that even if a pitch barely nicks an article of clothing, the batter is awarded first base. He summed up his philosophy like this: "Some people give their bodies to science; I give mine to baseball." Who was this scrappy man, who led the league in times hit by a pitch seven years in a row and a National League record 243 times over his career?

1. Minnie Minoso
2. Don Baylor
3. Ron Hunt
4. Frank Robinson

The answer is on page 34.

36. BATTER UP!

This long ball artist once said, only half-jokingly, "I don't break bats. I wear them out." Was it:

1. Babe Ruth
2. Jimmie Foxx
3. Josh Gibson
4. Willie Stargell

The answer is on page 34.

37. HIT IT All

One of this man's secrets to his hitting was that he could foul off pitches, even hard-to-handle inside ones, so he was unafraid to hit with two strikes on him. One reason he was so comfortable with two strikes was summed up by George Brett, who quipped, "A woman will be elected president before [he] is called out on strikes." What member of the 3,000 hit club and five-time batting champ was he referring to?

The answer is on page 34.

38. CONFIDENCE AND CONTROL

This man had total confidence in his bat control, believing he could handle any pitch, in any location. "Pitch me outside," he once said, "I will hit .400. Pitch me inside, and you will not find the ball." Who was this four-time batting champ?

The answer is on page 34.

39. PYTHON VS. PYTHON

In 1994, many fans felt this man would surely scorch 60-plus homers. He scoffed, telling the *Pittsburgh Post-Gazette* that sluggers such as Frank Thomas have "got those big pythons for arms. I've got little, skinny pythons. I can hit home runs, but I've got to get my whole little body behind it." What man, whose father also starred in the majors, was being rather modest as he later became a member of the 600 home run club in 2008?

The answer is on page 34.

40. FAILURE AND SUCCESS

He began by saying people recalled him for his home run hitting, but also for his numerous strikeouts. "The strikeout is the ultimate failure and I struck out 1,936 times—more than any player but Reggie Jackson. But I'm proud of my strikeouts too, for I feel that to succeed, one must first fail; and the more you fail, the more you learn about succeeding." Who is being quoted here?

1. Babe Ruth
2. Mike Schmidt
3. Willie Stargell
4. Willie McCovey

The answer is on page 34.

41. SEEING THE SIGNS

It was reported in an AP item that when this man was traded from the Phillies to the Angels he told Philadelphia manager Terry Francona that if he wound up facing his former team in the World Series he would "try to steal their signs," then confessed that that could present a problem for him because even when he was on the team, "I didn't know them." Clue: He was a powerful outfielder who, as a member of the Atlanta Braves, twice hit 30-plus homers while stealing more than 30 bases. His initials are R.G.

The answer is on page 34.

42. GOPHER THE HOME RUN CLUB

In 2004, one writer joked that there are 21, not the officially listed 20, members of the 500 home run club. He explained the extra man is pitcher Robin Roberts, who dished up 505 gopher balls during his long and excellent (Hall of Fame-caliber) career. What year did he finish his career with that staggering record for homers surrendered?

1. 1958
2. 1960
3. 1966
4. 1968

The answer is on page 35.

43. "BIG MAC" AND "THE BABE"

For years, the player who entered the 400 home run circle quicker than anyone was Babe Ruth. Not too long ago that changed when Mark McGwire took only 4,726 at bats (128 fewer than Ruth) to hit his 400th homer. When did "Big Mac" accomplish this?

1. 1996
2. 1997
3. 1998
4. 2000

The answer is on page 35.

44. WHAT GOES UP, MUST COME DOWN

Norm Cash stung the ball at a .361 pace one year then plunged to a .243 average the following season. That marked the sharpest one-year decline ever among players who qualified for the batting crown. His .361 batting average did win the crown, but the following year was brutal. When did he suffer through his dismal fall off to .243?

1. 1958
2. 1960
3. 1962
4. 1964

The answer is on page 35.

45. JAX'S RECORD

Fans thought Reggie Jackson was destined to eclipse Roger Maris' record for the most homers in a season when "Jax" got so hot he drilled 37 home runs by the All-Star break (four more than the previous record set by Maris by the '61 break). Guess which season Jackson set this unusual record:

1. 1967
2. 1969
3. 1971
4. 1974

The answer is on page 35.

46. HIGHS AND LOWS

One year Brady Anderson saw his home run total fall from 50 the previous season down to a mere 18, said to be the largest one-year nosedive ever. That same season featured Nomar Garciaparra driving home 98 runs to set the record for the most RBI ever by a leadoff hitter. When did these two events take place?

1. 1995
2. 1997
3. 2000
4. 2001

The answer is on page 35.

47. AMAZING STATS

Todd Helton was another post-Ted Williams hitter who came tantalizingly close to .400 one year. Playing for the Colorado Rockies in hitter-friendly Coors Field, he wound up hitting .372 to complement his 59 doubles, 42 HR, and his gaudy 147 RBI. Name the year Helton tore the cover off the ball:

1. 1998
2. 2000
3. 2001
4. 2002

The answer is on page 35.

◆ ◆ ◆

CAN YOU MAKE THE RIGHT CALL
FOR THESE FLY BALL PLAYS?

A simple fly ball to an infielder will bring a smile to a pitcher's face. Sometimes it can also lead to a lot of head scratching when things get a little more complicated. See if you will be smiling for knowing all the answers or scratching your head, like some of the players in these real examples.

48. CAUGHT

In the bottom of the ninth inning, the home team is trailing, 4–2, but has runners on first and second with two outs. A slugger comes to bat and hits a towering fly ball that stays in the infield. Is it an infield fly, making the game automatically over?

The answer is on page 35.

49. BUNTED

In extra innings, the home team has runners on first and second with no outs. Needing just one run to win, the batter tries to advance the runners with a sacrifice bunt. But he executes the bunt poorly and pops out to the catcher.

Is this an infield fly or could the catcher have let the ball drop and tried for two outs?

The answer is on page 36.

50. DROPPED

The bases are loaded with one out when the batter hits a short fly ball. The first baseman cannot hold onto the catch when the second baseman slams into him.

Is this an infield fly even though the ball was dropped?

The answer is on page 36.

51. MISSED

The bases are loaded with one out when the batter hits a pop fly in the infield. The ball, which could have been caught, eventually drops to the ground, untouched. A fielder picks the ball up and flips it to the catcher, who is standing on home plate. While the infielders congratulate themselves on an apparent double play, the runner from third crosses the plate.

Is this an infield fly? Is the runner from third out or is he safe at home?

The answer is on page 37.

52. IN THE OUTFIELD

With runners on first and second and one out, the batter hits a fly ball to short right field. The second baseman appears to settle under it, but at the last second he loses the ball in the sun and then falls over as the ball hits the grass. Once the runners see the second baseman fall, they advance to second and third.

Is this an infield fly even though the ball landed in the outfield?

The answer is on page 38.

53. NO SAFE PLACE TO STAND

Here's a play that is a definite infield fly. With runners on first and second and one out, the batter hits a pop fly toward second base. But the second baseman fails to catch the ball, which strikes the runner who is standing on second. We know that the batter is out on the infield fly, but there is one remaining question:

Is the lead runner called out for interference?

The answer is on page 39.

♦ ♦ ♦

HOME RUN, HUH?

See if you can solve the confusion caused by the detours these balls took before clearing the fence.

54. A STAR IS BORN

In the eighth inning of an interleague game, the home team is winning 3–1 and has a runner on base when an untested rookie steps to the plate. The batter hits the ball deep to left field. Uncertain where it will land, he runs quickly around the bases, finally scoring before he realizes that the ball had cleared the fence on a fly in fair territory.

Is this a home run?

The answer is on page 40.

55. PREMATURE CELEBRATION

The score is tied, 3–3, in extra innings when the home team loads the bases with one out. The batter hits an apparent grand slam home run over the fence, but is so excited that he and the runner from first base stop in their tracks and celebrate together. The rest of the team joins them, and the two runners never complete the trip around the bases. Meanwhile, the runners from second and third have gone around to score.

Is this a home run and what is the final score of the game?

The answer is on page 40.

56. BACK TO HOME

After a batter hits the ball over the fence for a home run, he runs to first base, but then turns around and jogs the rest of the way around the bases facing backward.

Is this allowed?

The answer is on page 42.

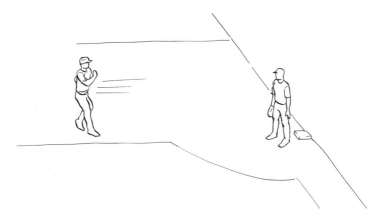

Chapter 1
ANSWERS

1. Vladimir Guerrero.

2. David Ortiz.

3. Rafael Palmeiro, joining Hank Aaron, Willie Mays, and Eddie Murray.

4. Harvey Kuenn. Amazingly, both times Kuenn made the final out was in no-hitters featuring Sandy Koufax on the mound—in the second instance, the no-no was, in fact, a perfect game.

5. "Slammin" Sammy Sosa.

6. Mel Ott, yet another Hall of Famer. Ott was his league's top home run hitter six times after breaking into the Major Leagues as a 17-year-old.

7. Honus Wagner of the Pittsburgh Pirates. As a trivia note, Wagner became the first player to have his signature branded into a Louisville Slugger bat back in 1905. Wagner is also noted for having hit over .300 for 17 straight seasons, beginning in 1897 when he was a mere rookie.

8. Hank Aaron, most famous, of course, for shattering Ruth's lifetime home run record of 714—Aaron ended his magnificent career with 755 shots.

9. Mark McGwire, who broke the former single season home run record of 61 when he crushed 70 homers in 1998 (only to see Barry Bonds breeze by that total in 2001 with 73 blows).

10. Mike Schmidt, one of a few men to win back-to-back MVP Awards. Schmidt entered the Hall of Fame when he received 444 votes out of 460 ballots cast in 1995. The Hall of Fame website boasts of Schmidt possessing "an unprecedented combination of power and defense . . ." By the time his career ended, he had punished the ball 548 times for home runs, and his 48 homers in 1980 remain the most ever in a season by a third sacker.

11. Rod Carew. Only Ty Cobb (with 12, the all-time high), Tony Gwynn, and Honus Wagner own more batting titles than his seven. He also reached the .300 level 15 years in a row.

12. Joe DiMaggio. Also known as the "Yankee Clipper," DiMaggio was a three-time MVP winner but probably remains most famous for his astonishing record 56-game hitting streak accomplished in 1941.

13. Yogi Berra, also a three-time AL MVP winner.

14. Ted Williams. Clearly he was a tremendous hitter for both power (521 lifetime blows) and average (.344 career; only seven men— most of them from the early days of the game—hit higher than Williams, including Ty Cobb's best-ever .367).

15. Babe Ruth hit the first-ever Yankee Stadium round-tripper, helping the Yanks knock off the Red Sox. Ruth also homered in his final Opener in 1935 when he made his NL debut with the Boston Braves.

16. The first DH ever was Ron Bloomberg of the New York Yankees and the date was April 6, 1973.

17. Hank Aaron hit his 714th homer off Billingham to tie Babe Ruth's lifetime total.

18. Dwight Evans was the first man to blast the season's first offering for a home run.

19. Frank Robinson, with eight home runs, ranks first for lifetime Opening Day circuit shots.

20. The first man to reach the 30, 40, 50, and throw in the 60 home run level, was the king of clout, Babe Ruth.

21. Babe Ruth began with C. the Boston Red Sox. Aaron started with A. the Milwaukee Braves. Bonds was originally a member of B. the Pittsburgh Pirates. Mays' trek through the majors began in the uniform of E. the New York Giants. And Robinson started out with D. the Cincinnati Reds.

22. Larry Walker began with D. the Montreal Expos. Casey started as a member of C. the Cleveland Indians. The Minnesota Twins E. gave Carew his first shot in the Bigs. Palmeiro was originally a Chicago Cub B. A-Rod's big league origin was with A. the Seattle Mariners.

23. Dick Sisler's homer won the NL flag for St. Louis.

24. Williams' manager the year he hit .406 was Joe Cronin.

25. The reviled player Lajoie had nearly snatched the crown from was Ty Cobb. Not only that, the day after Lajoie banged out his eight hits, seemingly enough to win the title, he received a congratulatory telegram from eight of Cobb's teammates—that's how deeply Cobb was hated!

Decades later the issue still wasn't totally resolved as researchers discovered Cobb had accidentally been given credit for two hits he had not really earned that year. Due to a double entry of statistics from a game in which he had gone 2-for-3, Cobb's listed average was higher than Lajoie's, but truly it wasn't. Still, to this day, although some sources differ as to the exact numbers these men put up, the official record book shows Cobb, with a .385 batting average, to be the batting champ of 1910.

26. It was Cecil Fielder, and he did this in 1991.

27. Hank Aaron, a man who lashed his bat with the speed and raw danger of Indiana Jones' bullwhip. Sparky Anderson praised Aaron's "fast hands and powerful wrists."

28. Cy Young, with 511 wins, ranks the number one of all time. The nearest pitcher to him was Walter Johnson and he was almost 100 wins behind Young at 417.

Scott Rolen was in awe of Cy Young's record."Unbelievable the amount of wins that he had. I mean, that's the most amazing, I think, to me." Simple math reveals a pitcher who begins at as early of an age as, say, 19 could win 25 games every single season of his career through the age of 38 and he'd still be shy of Young's total.

Not only that, with today's five-man pitching rotations, winning 25 is nearly an impossible feat for any given single season, let alone for 20 years in a row. The last time a pitcher notched 25 or more wins was in 1990 when Bob Welch did it for the A's.

29. Mark Whitten. He drove in 12 runs to tie the mark of Jim Bottomley. Interestingly, the man sometimes labeled "Hard Hittin' Mark Whitten" only hit 105 homers over 11 big league seasons. In all, only 11 men from the modern era have ever hit four homers during a nine-inning contest, including Lou Gehrig and Willie Mays.

The sensational Scott Rolen said of Whitten's home run outburst, "That's incredible, I don't know if it's chance or what it might be, but, I mean, that doesn't happen—it just doesn't happen! And twelve RBIs, that's a month right there in one game!"

30. It was popular first baseman Don Mattingly who powered six grand slams in 1987.

31. Julio Franco. In 2007, Franco retired at the age of 49.

32. Seattle's Ichiro Suzuki, who also holds the record for the most singles in a season (225).

33. Roger Maris, who hit 61 HR in 1961, was the first man to top Ruth.

34. Rogers Hornsby.

35. It was Ron Hunt who was willing to lean into the ball, even to the point of allowing himself to get plunked by a pitch in an Old-Timers Game! He held the all-time record for getting hit by pitches for quite some time. He said of ace pitchers who threw wicked fastballs, "If they throw too hard, I'll take one for the team. If you can't hit them, let them hit you."

Ironically, while beanballs never fazed him, "the only time I really got hurt was when Denver Lemaster hit my hamstring. I turned and tried to keep my balance."

36. Josh Gibson. The standout from the Negro League was enormously strong and hit some still-talked-about tape measure shots during his career.

37. Wade Boggs.

38. Roberto Clemente, a great bad ball hitter.

39. Ken Griffey, Jr.

40. 3. Willie Stargell.

41. Ron Gant.

42. 3. Roberts served up his last round-tripper in 1966. The most he gave up in a season was an inflated 46 in 1956, then the all-time single season record.

43. 3. McGwire hit his 400th homer on May 9, 1998.

44. 3. Cash's off year was 1962. He went on to become a solid but unspectacular .271 lifetime hitter over his 17-year big league career who never again sniffed a batting crown. His second highest average had been in 1960 when he hit a modest .286.

45. 2. Jackson's torrid first half came in 1969; he finished the season with 47 homers, far off his earlier record pace.

46. 2. Anderson's decline and Garciaparra's RBI record both took place in 1997.

47. 2. Helton's sterling season mentioned was 2000. The American League had two other players that also reached .372 around the same time. First, there was Nomar Garciaparra of the Red Sox who hit that stellar average in 2000, and then Ichiro Suzuki during his remarkable 2004 season with the Mariners. A fellow National Leaguer, Barry Bonds, came close with .370 in 2002 with the Giants.

48. ANSWER: Not an infield fly, because there are already two outs. The game is not over until the ball is caught.
GAME: In the second-longest rain-delayed game ever recorded, the New York Mets were hosting the San Francisco Giants on a damp Saturday afternoon in 1994. The 1,500 fans who waited the whole seven hours to the bitter end witnessed home runs by the Giants' Matt Williams and Barry Bonds, the two National League home run leaders at the time.

Despite losing Bobby Bonilla in a seventh-inning ejection, the Mets seemed like they might pull off a miracle victory in the bottom of the ninth. Hits by Jeromy Burnitz and David Segui put runners on first and second when Jeff Kent came to bat. Kent had hit home runs in his previous at-bat and in the previous game. This time, he was not so successful. He hit a fly ball to the infield off pitcher Rod Beck to end the game. Because there were already two outs, this was not an infield fly.

Mets manager Dallas Green was unlucky enough to have also participated in the longest ever rain-delayed game when he managed the Philadelphia Phillies in 1980. In that game, it took five hours for the rain to clear. The Giants were also the visiting team on that day.

49. ANSWER: Not an infield fly. The catcher could have tried to start a double play if he had let the ball drop and then thrown to second or third base.

GAME: In one of the most dramatic playoff games in recent times, the Boston Red Sox, facing elimination, took the New York Yankees to extra innings for the second game in a row. In the 2004 American League Championship Series, the Yankees had taken a 3–0 lead in games. Boston rallied in the fourth game to win on a David Ortiz home run in the 12th inning. In the fifth game, Boston once again came from behind, scoring two runs in the eighth inning to tie the score, 4–4.

The Red Sox opened the bottom of the 11th with singles by Bill Mueller and Mark Belhorn. Johnny Damon then tried a sacrifice bunt to move the runners forward. When he popped out to the catcher for the first out of the half-inning, the umpires did not call an infield fly because it was an attempted bunt rather than a full swing. In any case, the inning ended soon after when Orlando Cabrera grounded into a double play.

The Red Sox finally won the contest in the 14th inning and went on to win the next two games to reach the World Series, where they secured their first championship in 86 years.

50. ANSWER: Yes, it is an infield fly.

GAME: This play illustrates how chaos lurks behind every routine play in baseball. Mike Sweeney of the host Kansas City Royals hit a simple pop fly against Kyle Lohse of the Minnesota Twins with one out and the bases loaded early in the 2004 season. First baseman Doug Mientkiewicz appeared to catch the ball when second baseman Michael Cuddyer plowed into him and knocked the ball loose. The umpires had already signaled an infield fly, retiring Sweeney for the second out of the half-inning.

Unsure of whether he was safe or out, Sweeney planted himself on first base. As Desi Relaford tried to score from third, Mientkiewicz gathered up the ball and fired home, but pegged Sweeney in the back. Meanwhile, Royal runner Carlos Beltran took off toward second base where teammate Angel Berroa was standing motionless.

Twins catcher Henry Blanco chased after the ball, now rolling in foul territory, as Beltran headed back toward first base. Blanco then threw to quick-thinking right fielder Jacque Jones, who was covering the bag. Jones tagged Beltran for the third out.

The only remaining question was whether Relaford's run would count. Because there was no force play in effect and because the batter did not make the third out, this was a timing play. Relaford crossed the plate before the third out, so his run stood. This was Kansas City's third and final run in an 8–3 loss to Minnesota.

51. **ANSWER:** Yes, it is an infield fly. The runner from third is safe.
   GAME: Playing at home in this 2003 contest against the Montreal Expos, San Francisco Giant batter Barry Bonds hit a pop fly that did not make it as far as the pitcher's mound before it fell back to earth. The umpires called it an infield fly, which retired Bonds and removed the force. But a late gust of wind affected the ball, and it hit the ground.

At this point, confusion reigned. When Expo catcher Michael Barrett stepped on the plate with the ball, his action was meaningless because there was no longer a force. Crafty San Francisco runner Neifi Perez acted like he had been put out, but continued to walk home until he touched the plate and the umpire ruled him safe.

By the end of the inning, the Giants had tallied four runs to even the score. The Expos recovered, however, and won, 6–4.

Not one to learn from his mistakes, Barrett did the exact same thing later that year in a game against the Atlanta Braves. Once again thinking that the force remained in effect on the infield fly, Barrett stepped on the plate instead of tagging runner Robert Fick. He then threw to Todd Zeile at third base, where Vinny Castilla arrived safely for the same reason. That day, the Expos were punished for their infield fly illiteracy and lost, 10–6.

52. ANSWER: Yes, it is an infield fly.

GAME: In the Washington Nationals' first-ever spring training game in 2005, Washington batter Brendan Harris felt he should have been standing on first base when he advanced team-mates Jeffrey Hammonds and Terrmel Sledge on this infield fly. New York Mets second baseman Danny Garcia was charged with an error when both he and the ball fell to earth. The Nationals ended up stranding Hammonds and Sledge, but won the game, 5–3.

CALL: The first thing to remember about the infield fly is that the rule is designed to protect the runners. On a routine pop fly that an infielder should be able to catch, it would be unfair if the defense had the option of letting the ball drop in order to record a quick double play. This situation applies when there are fewer than two outs and runners on first and second or first, second, and third. If there are two outs already, then there is no risk of a double play. And if runners are in any other configuration, there is minimal risk of one (considering that the batter should be able to reach first if the pop fly is dropped).

An infield fly does not apply on an attempted bunt, because a bunt is a situation in which the offense no longer deserves protection from a double play. The expected outcome of a bunt with runners on base is one out; it is a sacrifice whose purpose is to advance the lead runners. If the infield fly protected the batting team from a double play on a bunt, then the batter would have nothing to lose by trying.

There is no artificial boundary on an infield fly. The rule has a misleading name, much like a "foul tip" which may be tipped by the batter but is not foul. Similarly, an infield fly can be a fly ball to the outfield. It should more accurately be called an "infielder fly," because the rule applies to a fly ball that can be caught by an infielder (although it may actually be caught by an outfielder or, as in some cases above, not caught at all).

Umpires cannot wait to see if a fielder actually catches the ball before they call an infield fly, because by waiting so long they would not be offering any protection to the runners. The offense may feel victimized by this when the defense commits an error, but this is a judgment call, and it is better for an umpire to call the batter out and prevent an unearned double play than to let chaos break loose. One rule of thumb is to check the runners. If they are running, then it is likely that they do not consider the fly ball to be a routine catch. In the example of the Nationals versus the Mets, the runners waited to see if the ball fell before they advanced. So even though the batter and all runners would have advanced safely on the play, the umpires could not gamble that there would be an error.

On an infield fly, the batter is automatically out, removing the force. Runners can advance if they want, but must tag up if the ball is caught. The ball remains alive.

53. **ANSWER:** No.
GAME: In 1997, this rare type of infield fly happened when the Seattle Mariners were visiting the Boston Red Sox. Jay Buhner was on first and Edgar Martinez was on second when Seattle batter Paul Sorrento hit the infield fly straight into Martinez. Not realizing he was protected when on base during an infield fly, Martinez assumed that he too was out when the ball hit him and he walked off the base. Alert Boston shortstop Nomar Garciaparra picked up the ball and tagged Martinez to end the half-inning. Despite the setback, the Mariners won, 5–3.

CALL: This is one of those crazy plays that was not covered by the rule book until it actually happened. Legend has it that Al Somers, the author of the apparent "fourth out" was the first umpire to face this situation. Somers ruled that because the infield fly is designed to protect the runners by allowing them to stay on their bases without the threat of a force out, it would be unfair for those runners to be called out for interference while remaining on base.

Normally, runners are out for interference when a hit ball (ground ball or fly ball) strikes them before passing an infielder. This applies even when the runners are on base. In short, the fielders have first rights to a batted ball, and runners must get out of the way or risk being called out for interference. The only exception is during an infield fly.

The home run might be the most awesome play in baseball. Yet the term home run is not defined in the rulebook and does not even appear in the index. Instead, it is covered by a number of different rules that, separately, govern batters and runners, and are mutually contradictory and incomplete. Perhaps for this reason, there are all sorts of confusing situations that can arise when the ball takes a few detours before going over the fence and when the batter does strange things on the way home.

54. ANSWER: Yes.

GAME: Well, obviously this is a home run, so consider this a bonus question. On June 15, 2005, 23-year-old Seattle Mariner rookie Mike Morse hit his first Major League home run. He did it against Ryan Madson of the Philadelphia Phillies and helped the Mariners on their way to a 5–1 victory.

CALL: You think all the home run questions will be this easy. Think again.

55. ANSWER: Not a home run. The final score is 4–3.

GAME: This intriguing play was one of the greatest post-season comebacks in the history of the New York Mets—a team that has won its share of exciting October games. Trailing 3–2 against the visiting Atlanta Braves in the bottom of the 15th inning of Game 5 of the 1999 National League Championship Series, the Mets put together a dramatic rally. With the help of a lead-off single by Shawon Dunston and walks by Matt Franco, John Olerud, and Todd Pratt, New York had tied the score and loaded the bases.

Needing no more than a base hit or sacrifice fly to win the game, batter Robin Ventura hit a Kevin McGlinchy pitch over the fence. Pinch-runner Roger Cedeno scored from third, Olerud scored from second, and Ventura and Pratt both stopped around second base to celebrate. The game ended with the score 4–3 on this memorable "grand slam single." The last laugh went to the Braves, however, who won the next game and advanced to the World Series.

CALL: Normally, in the bottom of the ninth or in extra innings, a game is over the moment the home team takes the lead. The exception to this is a game-ending home run, when all runners are permitted to score even if preceding runners have already taken the lead and effectively settled the outcome of the game. Had Pratt and Ventura continued around the bases, completing the home run, then the final score would have been 7–3. As it was, the fact that Ventura did not score meant that the play was not a home run, and so the game ended the moment the Mets took the lead, when Cedeno scored.

During the play, Ventura could have been called out for two separate reasons, either for passing Pratt or for abandoning his effort around the bases. Pratt could also have been called out for not continuing to run. The intriguing aspect of this play is that the Mets scored the go-ahead run and the third out was recorded (if we consider both Ventura and Pratt to have been out). In an apparent paradox, the game was over when Cedeno crossed the plate, but the game could have continued were it not for the fact that Ventura and Pratt abandoned their efforts. In effect, Olerud's run was withdrawn.

Matters could have become very thorny had either Ventura or Pratt failed to advance at least one base on the play. For example, if Pratt had stopped running and begun his celebrations before touching second base, then his out would have been a force out, and no run can score when the third out is a force out. Cedeno's run would not have counted, and the game might still be going on today. It would have taken a very brave umpire to nullify a game-winning grand slam in the playoffs over a technicality, but the Mets took an unnecessary risk when two runners abandoned their efforts around the basepaths.

There was a similar play in 2005, when the Milwaukee Brewers defeated the Cincinnati Reds, 6–5, in the bottom of the ninth on an apparent ground-rule double that bounced over the outfield wall. With the score tied and the bases loaded with no outs, Damian Miller hit a ball that hit the ground and continued into the outfield bleachers. Carlos Lee scored the winning run from third. Lyle Overbay did not bother to run all the way home from second. But even if he had, it would not have counted since the game was already over. Miller's hit was scored as a single.

56. **ANSWER:** Yes, but it looks silly.
GAME: Jimmy Piersall of the 1963 New York Mets had a mental illness that, by his own admission, made him more famous than did his mediocre baseball abilities. His agonizing career was portrayed by *Psycho*-star Anthony Perkins in the 1957 movie *Fear Strikes Out*. Before the construction of Shea Stadium, the Mets played their home games in the Polo Grounds, which had very short fences down the line. Piersall's homer—his first in two years and the 100th of his career—traveled a mere 258 feet. Since 1959, all new Major League ballparks must have fences at least 325 feet from home plate. But for the older parks, according to the rulebook, a fair ball hit over a fence at least 250 feet away is a home run.

For no good reason, Piersall ran most of the way around the bases with his rear leading the way. Despite the annoyance of the Philadelphia Phillies pitcher Dallas Green, there is nothing illegal about his play. The home run counted. Piersall's strange display did not go unpunished, however. Two days later, the Mets released him.

CALL: If a player runs around the bases clockwise in order to confuse the defense or to mock the game, then umpires will immediately call him out. But there is nothing in the rule book that says you must face forward when running the bases.

Chapter 2
Pitching

NAME THAT PITCHER!

1. PERFECTION

In 1965 Chicago Cubs pitcher Bob Hendley lost a 1–0 one-hitter. Hendley lost because I, a Los Angeles Dodgers pitcher, threw a perfect game that day. Only Lou Johnson's seventh inning double prevented this game from being a double no-hitter, something that has happened only once in the history of the game. In the fifth inning, Johnson had drawn a walk and scored after a sacrifice, a steal, and a Cubs error. Clue: I already had thrown three other no-hitters before my '65 masterpiece. Who am I?

The answer is on page 56.

2. HIT ME, I HIT YOU

I pitched alongside Sandy Koufax, once holding out with him in an unprecedented two-man power ploy to get a better contract from the Dodgers. Mike Shannon once spoke about my fearlessness and my willingness to brush back and even bean batters to get my message across that I was in control. He said that I "would consider an intentional walk a waste of three pitches. If he wants to put you on base, he can hit you with one." Who am I?

The answer is on page 56.

3. SUPERLATIVE SOUTHPAW

My "out" pitch was my sharp-as-a-straight-razor slider. I set a record with 19 strikeouts in a 1969 game (since broken), with many of the K's coming on sliders.

I attributed much of my success to grueling workouts, which included stretching, lifting, and martial arts work. Final clue: In 1972, even though my Philadelphia Phillies were a terrible team, I won an astounding 27 games, accounting for almost 50 percent of my team's measly 59 victories. Who am I?

The answer is on page 56.

4. FORMER KING OF K

For a baseball eon, my lifetime strikeout record stood insurmountable. Finally, it was toppled when Nolan Ryan fanned his 3,509th victim. They say my fastball is still among the swiftest of all time, and that, coupled with my sidearm delivery, helped me amass 110 shutouts, still the most ever. I spent 21 seasons with the Washington Senators and the last time I took the field, way back on September 30, 1927, was as a pinch-hitter (only six pitchers ever hit more than my 24 lifetime homers) in the same contest that Babe Ruth tagged his 60th home run. Final clue: I was one of the five charter members inducted into the Hall of Fame. Who am I?

The answer is on page 56.

5. WHAT A START!

Who is the only man to fire a no-hitter on Opening Day? He was a Cleveland Indians great and his performance took place in 1940 versus the White Sox. Name this man.

The answer is on page 56.

6. GIVE ME THE BALL

In 1985, this pitcher made his record-setting 15th Opening Day start. He retired with 16 in total—a record to this day. Name this three-time Cy Young Award winner, who was also the Rookie of the Year in 1967 with the Mets.

The answer is on page 57.

7. FATHER'S DAY MASTERPIECE

On Father's Day of 1964 (June 21), a Philadelphia Phillies pitcher threw a no-hitter to become the first man to record a no-hitter in both leagues. Who was this righty?

The answer is on page 57.

8. PERFECT ENDING

Back on September 30, 1984, an Angels pitcher tossed baseball's only perfect game on the final day of a season. The 6' 7" righty dazzled the Rangers that day, 1–0, using a scant 94 pitches and going to a three-ball count just once. His initials are M.W. Name this "perfectionist."

The answer is on page 57.

9. NOTCHING #300

This Hall of Fame pitcher reached his 300th win on the season finale in 1985. Facing the Blue Jays, this 46-year-old Yankees righty (who broke in with the Milwaukee Braves in 1964) worked a four-hit shutout. Clue: He didn't use his specialty pitch until the ninth inning, trying to prove he could win without his unusual pitch.

The answer is on page 57.

10. A FIRST AND A LAST

Who was the first ambidextrous pitcher in pro ball? The last one to date?

The answer is on page 57.

11. RAPID ROBERT

Bob Feller, also known as "Rapid Robert," once set a rather

offbeat but certainly laudatory record when he, as a 17-year-old, struck out 17 batters. For years, no pitcher ever managed to fan the number of men that matched his age until Kerry Wood whiffed 20 while pitching for the Chicago Cubs at the age of 20. When did this monumental performance take place:

1. 1996
2. 1998
3. 2000
4. 2001

The answer is on page 58.

12. SKY-HIGH ERA

Doug Drabek posted a 12–11 record one year while being saddled with a sky-high 5.74 ERA. That marked the highest ERA for an American League pitcher with a winning record in the annals of the league. What year was that:

1. 1992
2. 1995
3. 1996
4. 1997

The answer is on page 58.

13. BACK-TO-BACK NO-HITTERS

Johnny Vander Meer, working in just his second big league season, fired a no-hitter on June 11 for the Cincinnati Reds, topping the Boston Bees. Incredibly, in his next outing four days later, he matched his excellence, no-hitting the Brooklyn Dodgers by a 6–0 margin. No man has ever again achieved back-to-back no-hitters. When did Vander Meer spin his magic:

1. 1932
2. 1936
3. 1938
4. 1940

The answer is on page 58.

14. PITCHER DECEPTION

Pedro Martinez of the New York Mets is on the hill with enemy runners off first and third with, say, two outs. Martinez would like to get out of the inning the easy way, by picking off a runner rather than face the risk of offering up a juicy pitch to the batter. Is he permitted to fake a throw to third, swivel, and then fire the ball to first, perhaps catching a napping runner straying off the bag too far?

The answer is on page 58.

15. INFAMOUS BLUNDER

The host Brooklyn Dodgers took a 4–3 lead into the ninth inning against the Yankees during Game 4 of the 1941 World Series when suddenly things began to go terribly wrong for them. Brooklyn relief pitcher Hugh Casey, needing just one out to tie the Series at two wins apiece, ran the count against Tommy Henrich to 3–2. What took place on the next pitch?

The answer is on page 59.

16. GOPHER BALLS GALORE

This pitcher holds the negative record for surrendering the most home runs in a single season, 50. However, when it came to a real killer of a curve, they should have labeled his nasty breaking ball "Deadman's Curve" because that lethal pitch put so many hitters away. Who is he?

The answer is on page 59.

17. MR. DEPENDABLE

Through 2004, this pitcher has been the epitome of consistency, racking up 15 or more wins every season for 17 consecutive years. That eclipsed the former record held by the venerable Cy Young. Clue: The new record-holder has been with the Cubs twice, beginning his big league days there in 1986, and is a multiple winner of the Cy Young Award.

The answer is on page 59.

18. GERIATRIC CASE; ODD RECORD

In 2005, Pat Borders was salvaged from the scrap heap of disuse and old age in terms of baseball years. He was 42 when the Seattle Mariners signed him to a big league contract. During a game in May when the M's starting pitcher was also a 42-year-old, the two men made history as the oldest batterymates ever. Can you name this clever, soft-throwing hurler?

The answer is on page 59.

19. BLAZING FAST

This man fired his pitches with the speed and explosiveness of an avalanche. When he retired in 1993, he owned just about every important strikeout record on the books; and, for the most part, he still is recognized as the King of K's. For example, while Randy Johnson has continued his string of strikeout pyrotechnics into the 2000s, this man's career strikeout record of 5,714 could stand for a very long time.

Likewise, his seven no-hitters is a seemingly insurmountable record. Who is this fireballing phenom who struck out a record 383 men in 1973?

The answer is on page 59.

20. MONOPOLY ON THE CY YOUNG AWARD

Despite his age, this pitcher was still active and going strong until retiring in 2007. In the end, he owned 354 wins, with a tiny 3.12 ERA, versus only 184 defeats. In postseason play, he has still managed to win big; 60 percent of his decisions are victories. In addition, he has captured more Cy Young Awards (seven) than any other pitcher in the history of baseball.

The answer is on page 59.

21. HEARTBREAKER

What Brooklyn Dodger pitcher once gave up a homer to Tommy Henrich that resulted in him losing a 1–0 heartbreaker? He somehow managed to keep his sense of humor when reporters asked him what pitch he had thrown to Henrich. The hurler replied, "A change of space." Clues: This Dodgers player posted a lifetime 149–90 record and his initials are D.N.

The answer is on page 60.

22. SKILLS ARE JUST SKIN DEEP

Just going on his physical appearance, it was hard to believe this player was as skilled as he was. He once won 25 contests and fanned 308 batters, yet he possessed a potbelly physique. A hard worker who once averaged 330 innings pitched over a four-year span, this man joked, "A guy will be watching me on TV and see that I don't look in any better shape than he is.

'Hey, Maude,' he'll holler. 'Get a load of this guy. And he's a 20-game winner.'" Was this pitcher:

A) Rich Gossage

B) Mickey Lolich

C) Wilbur Wood

The answer is on page 60.

23. RE-SIGNING

In 1989, Yankees general manager Bob Quinn announced they had re-signed one of their pitchers. Quinn intoned to the media, "I would not preclude [him] from appearing in different roles." He was, of course, saying the pitcher might wind up working as both a starter and a reliever. The player, however, quipped, "I'm not going to be playing the role of Hamlet, am I?" Who said it? Clues: This southpaw enjoyed one of the finest single seasons of pitching ever in 1978 when he went 25–3, fired nine shutouts, posted a microscopic ERA of 1.74, and won nearly 90 percent of all his decisions.

The answer is on page 60.

24. BEST EYES IN THE BUSINESS

Who was pitcher Bobby Shantz referring to when he said he had been warned about pitching to this all-time great? "It was great advice," he began, "very encouraging. They said he had no weakness, won't swing at a bad ball, has the best eyes in the business, and can kill you with one swing; he won't hit at anything bad, but don't give him anything good." Big clue: The man being discussed was nicknamed "The Splendid Splinter."

The answer is on page 60.

25. DOC PITCHER

What all-time great, the consensus pick as the best leadoff man in the history of baseball, was pitcher Doc Medich talking about when he said, "He's like a little kid in a train station. You turn your back on him and he's gone."

The answer is on page 60.

26. PITCHED

In the sport of cricket, to "pitch" the ball is to throw it in such a way that it hits the "pitch," which is the word the English use for the ground. In baseball, a pitch that hits the ground is not a very good one. But what happens if the batter forgets which sport he is playing and swings at such a delivery?

If a batter swings and makes contact with a pitch after it has bounced, does the ball remain in play?

The answer is on page 60.

◆ ◆ ◆

CAN YOU CALL THESE BALKS?

There is probably no more mysterious rule in baseball than the balk. Sometimes the ball remains alive, sometimes it is dead. Announcers often have a hard time explaining what happened. The following pages provide three examples to test your balk literacy.

27. NO TIME

With a runner on second base, the pitcher is in the set position, ready to make the next pitch. Just as he starts his windup, the

batter asks for time. The umpire correctly refuses the request. But the pitcher becomes confused and halts his delivery.

Is this a balk?

The answer is on page 61.

28. OOPS

In a scoreless game, the visitors have runners on first and third with two outs. As the pitcher assumes the set position, he loses concentration for a moment and drops the ball to the ground. Neither runner was moving.

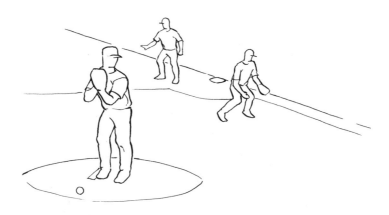

Is this a balk or, because the pitcher was standing on the rubber, is it called a "ball?"

The answer is on page 61.

29. FAKE-OUT

The score is tied 1–1 in the bottom of the 14th inning, and the home team has runners on first and third with one out. With no balls and two strikes on the batter, the pitcher believes that the runner from first will try to steal second, so he tries a pick-off move. The pitcher, using only his arm, fakes a throw to third base and then wheels around and steps and throws to first base.

Is this a balk?

The answer is on page 61.

Chapter 2
ANSWERS

1. Sandy Koufax, a man who had engineered no-hitters in 1962, 1963, and 1964, then topped it off with his perfecto. In that game, Koufax struck out 14, including six of the final seven Cubs hitters, lifting his record to 22–7. His four no-hitters stood as the all-time record until it was snapped by Nolan Ryan, who has seven. Hendley ended the year at 4–4 and was a sub-.500 pitcher lifetime (48–52).

2. "Double D," Don Drysdale, like Koufax, a Hall of Famer. Drysdale set a record in 1968 when he blanked opponents for 58 straight innings. In 1965, he led the Dodgers' entire team in batting when he was the only .300 hitter in their lineup. That same year, he tied his own National League record for the most homers hit in a season by a pitcher (seven).

3. 300-game winner Steve Carlton, owner of six 20-win seasons. He was also the first man to accumulate four Cy Young Awards and remains the second winningest southpaw ever, trailing only Warren Spahn.

4. Walter Johnson. His 417 career victories still stands second on the all-time list, trailing only Cy Young's 511 wins. Truly one of the best hitting pitchers ever, his astronomical .433 batting average in 1925, racked up very late in his career and, at the age of 37, set a still-untouched record for pitchers. For that matter, no everyday player has hit that high, either.

5. Bob Feller. His feat resulted in a peculiar bit of trivia—the no-hitter marked the first time ever that every hitter finished a game with exactly the same batting average he had coming into that contest, .000!

6. Tom Seaver had the 15 Opening Day starts.

7. Jim Bunning threw a no-hitter in the AL for Detroit and the 1964 classic with the Phillies. By the way, his catcher on that Father's Day, Gus Triandos, became the first man to have caught a no-hitter in both circuits.

8. Mike Witt threw the season-ending perfect game.

9. It was Phil Niekro, master of the knuckleball. He whipped out that pitch just three times in all, doing so when he whiffed the game's last batter, Jeff Burroughs. Niekro later commented in an autobiography, "I always wanted to pitch a whole game without throwing a knuckleball because people thought I couldn't get anyone out without doing so." As for his decision to unveil the pitch to secure his 300th win, he simply stated, "I figured there was no other way to finish the game than to use the pitch that got me there."

10. The first professional to pitch ambidextrously was Tony Mullane way back on July 18, 1882, while hurling for Louisville. Mullane, normally a righty, faced Baltimore, and when a batch of three straight lefties came to the plate, Mullane, according to a newspaper report of the day, "changed his delivery from right-handed to left, and puzzled the batters considerably."

The most recent pitcher who threw both ways in a big league game was Greg Harris of the Montreal Expos. As the 1995 season wound down, Harris, a natural righty (who was listed as a switch-hitter), became the second post-1900 pitcher to accomplish this feat. He worked a scoreless ninth inning of the September 28 game versus Cincinnati and did so using a specially constructed six-finger glove that allowed him to switch easily from one hand to the other.

Also, in the spring of 1990 a pitcher for St. Leo College in Florida started four games over a six-day span. What enabled him to toil so often was his ambidexterity.

As of 2008, Pat Venditte is pitching in the Yankee minor leagues with this rare talent.

11. 2. Wood blew away a record-tying 20 Houston Astros on May 6, 1998, pitching a one-hitter in which he allowed no walks. Remarkably, he managed this in just his fifth big league start (upping his record to 3–2).

In his next outing, Wood smashed the old record for the most strikeouts over a two-game span when he K'ed 13 Arizona batters. His 33 combined strikeouts toppled the old mark of 32 shared by Nolan Ryan, Randy Johnson, Dwight Gooden, and Luis Tiant, putting the rookie Wood in mighty fine company.

As a coincidental tidbit, Wood, a Texan just like Ryan and Clemens, wears the same jersey number as those two strikeout artists, men he said inspired him. Wood also said he didn't have good stuff when he was warming up, but during the game "felt like I was playing catch."

12. 4. Drabek's winning season with a steep ERA was in 1997. A National League pitcher, Guy Bush, went 15–10 for the Cubs in 1930 but registered an abysmal 6.20 ERA.

13. 3. Vander Meer's two masterpieces came in 1938, a year in which he went 15–10 overall.

14. While pitchers can't fake a throw to an empty base or, for that matter, fake a throw to first (those moves would be called balks), what is described here is perfectly legal but very, very rarely works.

However, veteran pitcher Wilson Alvarez said he's not only seen it succeed, but he played with an expert at it when he was with the Chicago White Sox. "Oh, yeah," he smiled, "I saw that play many times with Jack McDowell. He used to pick off like four or five guys a year like that. I think he was the best in the league at that." He went so far as to say that this play works more often than one might expect at the Major League level.

15. Casey unloaded a dirt-low pitch (some say it was a "fast-breaking curve") that neither Henrich nor Dodger catcher Mickey Owen could handle. Although Henrich swung and missed for what should have been the game-ending strikeout, after the ball skittered by Owen, Henrich reached first safely. The flood-gate opened and the Yanks thrived, rallying for four runs; the Dodgers never recovered, rolling over and dying in a five-game Series. Owen had committed only two passed balls that year, and many observers actually felt the blame belonged on Casey, contending that the pitch he had uncorked was actually a tough-to-handle spitball.

16. Bert Blyleven, winner of 279 games. As strange as it sounds, in 1986, the year he gave up his record 50 homers, he posted a fine 17–14 record. The following year, he generously issued an addi-tional 46 homers to tie for the second most given up in a season.

17. Greg Maddux. Every year he is good for almost exactly 200 innings of toil and throughout his long, illustrious career he has spent only one stint on the disabled list.

18. Jamie Moyer. Borders, by the way, is also the answer to another trivia item: He is the only player ever to win the MVP of the World Series (in 1992 with the Toronto Blue Jays) and an Olympic gold medal (as a member of the 2000 Team USA).

19. Nolan Ryan, also known as the Ryan Express, set the record for 383 strikeouts. Ryan's longevity was unmatched; he endured 27 years of violent deliveries to the plate, yet stayed remarkably healthy on route to his numerous records.

20. Roger Clemens.

21. Don Newcombe.

22. Mickey Lolich. He not only was a 20-game winner, in the 1968 World Series he came up big, winning a record-tying three games to guide his Tigers to the championship.

23. It was "Louisiana Lightning," Ron Guidry.

24. Ted Williams.

25. Rickey Henderson.

26. ANSWER: Yes, the ball is in play.

GAME: Late in the 2005 season, the Philadelphia Phillies and Houston Astros were battling for the National League wild card. With the Phillies ahead by half a game, the Astros arrived in Philadelphia for a crucial series.

In the first game, Houston led 4–2, when Philadelphia mounted a comeback in the bottom of the ninth. After scoring one run, the Phillies had runners on second and third with two outs. The next at-bat meant everything. A hit would win the game and an out would lose it.

The batter was Endy Chavez. Houston pitcher Brad Lidge threw a slider that bounced in front of home plate. Chavez swung, made contact, and hit a foul ball. On the next pitch, Chavez struck out, and the game was over.

Houston took the wild card lead that day and ended the season one game ahead of Philadelphia. Chavez's at-bat effectively decided the outcome of the season for both teams. Houston went on to the World Series, but lost to the Chicago White Sox.

CALL: Just as in cricket, there is no problem in baseball with hitting a pitch after it bounces. Chavez hit a foul ball. But had he put the ball in play, it would have been just like any other hit, and could even have been caught for an out.

27. ANSWER: No balk.

GAME: In a 2001 Cincinnati-Houston game, and on a play following an overthrow to first, Octavio Dotel failed to complete his pitch when he saw Reds batter Jason LaRue ask for time. After initially calling a balk, the umpires got together and decided to nullify the play. LaRue later popped out on a bunt for the first out of the half-inning.

Cincinnati manager Bob Boone threatened to protest the game over this decision, but it would not have made any difference. Pinch hitter Calvin Pickering hit a single that drove home Pokey Reese from second base. The Reds won the game, 3–2.

28. ANSWER: It's a balk.

GAME: Pitcher Kerry Wood of the Chicago Cubs was guilty of a costly dropped ball during a game against the Milwaukee Brewers in 2000. When the ball hit the ground, the umpires called a balk, scoring Ron Belliard from third base and moving Marquis Grissom to second base. Wood recovered and helped Chicago to a 4–2 victory.

29. ANSWER: It's a balk.

GAME: Some say that baseball is like chess, not in the sense that it is incredibly slow and boring but because managers are often thinking several moves ahead. In this particular game in 2004, Oakland A's manager Ken Macha tried to be so clever that he called for a play that was of limited potential benefit and ended up costing his team the game.

The strangeness began in the ninth inning, when the host Seattle Mariners blew a 1–0 lead by giving up a home run to Oakland's Jermaine Dye. Dye's blast would have been caught by Seattle's Ichiro Suzuki, except that a fan got in the way. The game was tied 1–1.

Almost five hours since the game began, the Mariners were threatening to score in the 14th, with Bret Boone on first and Quinton McCracken on third and one out. A's pitcher Justin

Duchscherer ran the count to 0–2 against Scott Spiezio.

In this situation, the Mariners had two priorities: score the runner from third and try to avoid a double play that would end the inning. The A's, on the other hand, were looking for outs and were desperate to stop the runner on third from scoring. Macha thought he had figured out a sneaky way to get an out by anticipating Seattle's focus on avoiding a double play. With an 0–2 count, he called for a fake throw to third base and a quick return throw to first base.

There were two problems with the execution of the play, however. First, the pitcher did not step toward third base during his fake throw. Second, the first baseman was not aware of the plan and was standing well off of his base, making it impossible to record an out there whatever happened.

In this dazzling display of move and countermove, the A's neglected their main priority of stopping a run from scoring. The umpires called a balk, and the game ended there and then.

Duchscherer is part of a long line of pitchers to have lost a game on a balk call. Others who have fallen victim to the so-called "balk-off" game-ending play are Matt Turner (causing the Florida Marlins to lose to the Atlanta Braves in 1993), Jeff Zimmerman (causing the Texas Rangers to lose to the Baltimore Orioles in 2000), John Rocker (causing the Braves to lose to the Marlins in 2000), and Taylor Buchholz (causing the Colorado Rockies to lose to the Atlanta Braves in 2008).

CALL: Here is not the place to describe the dozen-plus ways to balk. But by keeping in mind some basic ideas, you should be able to understand when a balk does or does not occur.

The balk is a penalty imposed when the defense gains an unfair advantage in deceiving a base runner through a violation of the rules, and it leads to a one-base award. This is a delayed dead ball, so that the offense is not penalized, if, for example, a batter hits a home run on an illegal pitch.

Most balk violations happen because a pitcher fails to do one of the three things he must do if he is standing on the rubber with runners on base: pitch the ball (following a complete stop with his hands together, if he is in the set position); step and throw to an occupied base (or, in the case of second and third bases, he can step and fake a throw); or step backwards off the rubber while separating his hands. Failure to do one of these three things will result in a balk.

Once a pitcher steps off the rubber, he is free of these obligations and can do almost anything (except pitch or pretend to pitch). He can throw to an unoccupied base, fake a throw to first base, throw without stepping toward a base, drop the ball, and so forth.

Following these guidelines, two of the balk calls are obvious. When Wood dropped the ball, he did something that was not one of his three obligations. (Had he dropped the ball so wildly that it crossed a foul line, then it would have been considered a pitch and almost certainly a "ball.") Likewise, when Duchscherer faked to third base without stepping in that direction, he committed a balk.

Dotel's non-balk is not so clear, however. He also failed to perform one of the three obligations, but in his case it was not his fault, so the balk was not called. The rulebook states that batters will not be granted time when a pitcher is in the set position or has started a delivery. If a batter steps out of the box, then the pitch will count. To protect pitchers from batters who try to distract them, the rules also state that when a batter steps out of the box and causes a pitcher to balk, then both infractions will be ignored and the play will not count.

On Dotel's halted delivery, however, LaRue remained in the box, which is why Boone considered protesting the call. But the rules go further and say that no balk can be called when a member of the offensive team calls "time" for the purposes of trying to induce a balk. If the umpires thought that LaRue was purposefully trying to cause a balk, then they would have ejected him from the game. In this case, they decided that his deception was unintentional but still unfair to the pitcher. The umpires applied their common sense and nullified the play.

Chapter 3

Base Running

THE RIGHT WAY

1. DRAMATIC ENDING

Reliever Mike Stanton was with the Atlanta Braves in 1992 when they won the National League pennant. His most unforgettable moment in the majors was when a teammate of his "scored on that ground ball in the hole [and into left field]. There's no way he should've scored as slow as [he] runs. And Barry Bonds comes up on the ball so fast [in the outfield], so good, but," he concluded in an announcer-like dramatic voice, "Braves go to the Series."

Braves catcher Javy Lopez added, "Francisco Cabrera got that base hit and I was in the bullpen. It was amazing that he got that hit to beat the Pirates." He was correct—Cabrera had very few moments of fame in the majors, lasting only 196 games and driving in just 62 runs, but baseball fans will forever remember his name. However, can you recall the slow player who managed to beat Bonds' throw to the plate to score the dramatic run? Clue: his initials are S.B.

The answer is on page 75.

2. WHAT A SHOT!

During the 1989 American League Championship Series, a slugger for the Oakland A's teed off on a pitch and propelled it way up into the fifth level at Toronto's Skydome. Todd Hundley called that colossal shot "the most amazing thing I ever saw. That was a bomb!" While other homers have traveled greater distances—Mark McGwire hit one further in the same park, for instance—this homer got off the bat so fast and soared so high during a vital game, it is still spoken of in hushed tones today. Who spanked that long drive? Clue: He was also the first man to steal 40 or more bases while hitting 40-plus homers in a season.

The answer is on page 75.

3. FUNNY, BUT YOU'RE STILL OUT

An amusing play took place when a future Hall of Famer, known for his power and certainly not for his speed, took off from first base on a hit-and-run play. When the batter swung through the pitch, the lumbering runner slid, but came up about six feet short of the second base bag. Coming up from his slide, and seeing the enemy shortstop was about to apply a tag, the dead duck runner smiled sheepishly at the umpire, formed a T with his hands, and called "Time out!" Needless to say, he was called out. Who was this all-time Pirate great?

The answer is on page 75.

4. DOES CRIME PAY?

Rickey Henderson, the greatest base burglar of all time, set a single season record with 130 in 1982, a dozen more than previous record-holder Lou Brock had managed. However, one year Henderson also established the record for the most times being caught stealing in a season, 42 times. What year did this occur?

1. 1978
2. 1980
3. 1982
4. none of these

The answer is on page 75.

◆ ◆ ◆

ON INTERFERENCE

Inevitably, base runners and defensive players will cross paths on the baseball diamond. Players and fans have also been known to clash. In such cases, it's important to know who has the right to be somewhere and who is in the wrong.

5. STAY IN LANE

The batter hits a "squibber"—a weak ground ball that is fielded by the catcher. On the way to first base, the batter runs with one foot on the infield side of the 45-foot running lane. The catcher's throw is high, and the batter makes it to first base safely.

Is the batter out for interference?

The answer is on page 75.

DEFINITION: INTERFERENCE PART 1 (OFFENSIVE)

It is offensive interference when a member of the batting team illegally prevents a fielder from making a play.

6. ALTER COURSE

Leading off an inning, a batter hits the ball to center field and tries to stretch his hit into a double. While rounding first, however, he has to alter course slightly in order to avoid colliding with the first baseman, who is watching the ball. Sliding into second, he is tagged out on a close play.

Is this considered interference, obstruction, or neither? If one of the two, what is the penalty?

The answer is on page 76.

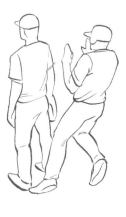

DEFINITION: OBSTRUCTION

Obstruction is when a member of defensive team, while not holding the ball or fielding the ball, slows the advance of a runner.

7. CRASH

With a runner on first base and two outs, the batter hits a routine ground ball to the second baseman. But the second baseman fields the ball directly in the basepath between first and second, and the runner from first makes contact with him.

Who had the right of way in this instance, and who is guilty of obstruction or interference? What is the penalty?

The answer is on page 77.

8. GOING BACK

Now that you have mastered the basics of obstruction and interference from the previous two questions, here's a twist on the scenario:

Caught in a rundown between third and home, a base runner is chased back to third by the catcher. The catcher throws to the shortstop, covering the bag, but in the meantime, the runner collides with the third baseman, who is standing in his way.

Is this interference or obstruction, and what is the penalty?

The answer is on page 78.

9. SLIDING INTO NOWHERE

With runners on first and third and one out, the batter hits a ground ball for a possible double play. After the shortstop touches second base holding the ball, he steps away from the bag in order to make a clear throw to first. But the runner from first tries to break up the double play by sliding underneath the shortstop, even though this means his slide takes him away from the base. In the end, the runner's slide has no effect on the throw to first, which was too late to complete the double play.

Is this interference on the part of the runner from first base, even though the batter would have made it to first base anyway?

The answer is on page 81.

10. SLAP-HAPPY

A runner stands on first base with one out when the batter hits a ground ball up the first base line. The pitcher fields the ball and tries to tag the batter. But the batter slaps the ball out of the pitcher's glove. The ball rolls all the way to the outfield, allowing the runner from first to score and the batter to reach second base.

Is this a legal play or is it interference?

The answer is on page 81.

11. BLIND SPOT

The home team has runners on first and third with one out in a game that is tied in extra innings. The batter hits a fly ball to left field, just about far enough to become a sacrifice fly that could score the winning run. The runner on third has trouble seeing the catch because the shortstop is blocking his view. After the catch, the runner takes a few steps toward home and then retreats to the safety of third base.

Is this obstruction and should the runner be awarded home plate?

The answer is on page 83.

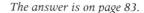

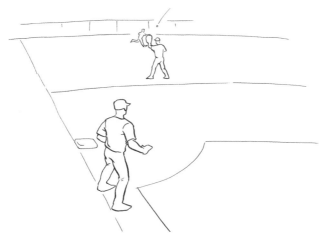

12. DEFLECTED

The home team is trailing by two runs in the bottom of the ninth with two outs and the bases loaded. The batter hits a fair ball into the left field corner, where a fan leans over and tries to grab it. He does not hold on, and the ball glances off his hand and deflects back into fair territory.

Is this interference and, if so, how many runs can score on the play?

The answer is on page 83.

13. STOLEN

In the eighth inning of a playoff game, trailing by one run, a batter for the home team hits a deep fly ball toward the right field fence. The right fielder arrives to make the catch, and just as the ball appears to reach the top of the wall, a fan swipes it for himself.

Is this a home run or an automatic out?

The answer is on page 84.

14. CURSED

Also in the eighth inning of a playoff game, the visiting team is behind by three runs with one out and a man on second. The batter hits a foul pop close to the seats down the third base line. The left fielder, reaching over the fence, has a good chance at the catch, but the ball is deflected away by a fan in the front row.

Is this a foul ball or an automatic out?

The answer is on page 84.

DEFINITION: INTERFERENCE PART 2 (SPECTATOR)

It is spectator's interference (also fan interference) when a spectator reaches onto the field or enters the field and touches a live ball or gets in the way of a player. When a person who is authorized to be on the field (like a security guard or ball boy) gets in the way, then it is only interference if it is intentional.

Chapter 3
ANSWERS

1. Sid Bream.

2. Jose Canseco.

3. Willie Stargell.

4. 3. Henderson was gunned out 42 times the same year he stole his 130 bases, 1982.

5. **ANSWER:** He is out for interference.

GAME: The New York Yankees were visiting the Toronto Blue Jays in 2004 when this play occurred. After fielding a weak ground ball by Blue Jay Alex Rios, Yankee catcher Jorge Posada threw high to first base. Even though the throw did not hit the runner, Rios caused Posada to alter the trajectory of the attempted put-out when he ran outside of his running lane. Rios was called out for interference in a game that New York won, 7–4, after having trailed 4–0.

Perhaps the most famous play involving these mysterious lines in the second half of the route to first base occurred in the second game of the 1998 American League Championship Series between the Yankees and the Cleveland Indians. Cleveland's Travis Fryman bunted in the 12th inning with the score tied, 1–1. New York first baseman Tino Martinez threw to Chuck Knoblauch, covering the bag, but the ball hit Fryman in the back as he was running outside of the lane, on the infield grass.

In this case, the umpires did not call interference, even though replays showed that Fryman ran the entire 45 feet outside of the running lane. This was a rare umpiring gaffe, but one that was not quite so destructive as the one Knoblauch made on the play. Instead of running after the ball, Knoblauch remained at first base to argue the umpire's decision. In the meantime, Enrique Wilson scored the go-ahead run and Fryman made it to second base. Later, Knoblauch might have discussed this play with teammate David Cone, who had some experience arguing with umpires while his opponents rounded the bases. The Indians soon won the game, 4–1, but lost the series, 4–2.

CALL: Years ago, before I became an umpire, while watching a minor league game in Maine, I asked no one in particular: What is the meaning of that lane on the second half of the baseline between home and first? A local fan turned around and said sarcastically that I must be new to baseball. In fact, I had watched the game for years, but I never understood the rules that apply to the lane until I went to umpire school.

The lane, which is on the foul-territory side of the first-base line, makes it possible for the batter to run to first base without risking interference. On a bunt or short ground ball, the fielder will have to throw the ball around the runner. If the runner has one or both of his feet outside of the three-foot-wide lane, then he should be called out for interference if his body gets in the way of the throw. If he is entirely within the lane and the throw hits him, then the ball remains in play.

The ball must actually be thrown for there to be interference, but it does not actually have to hit the runner. Many times, I have seen a pitcher or catcher hold back from throwing to first base when the runner is clearly outside of the running lane. All they would need to do is throw the ball, and the runner would be called out. The umpire does not need to judge whether the runner would have been out were it not for the interference. If there is interference, there will be an out. It really does pay for players to know the rules!

6. **ANSWER:** Obstruction. The runner is awarded second base.
   GAME: In 2000, the Yankees and Mets faced off at Shea Stadium in the first game of a rare day-night doubleheader in which both teams hosted a game. This unusual situation, which saw an estimated

30,000 fans use the subway to go from one stadium to the other, came about following a rainout earlier in the season. The nightcap at Yankee Stadium would be remembered for Yankee pitcher Roger Clemens's beaning of Met catcher Mike Piazza in the head. But in the first game, controversy surrounded the very first pitch.

Yankee Chuck Knoblauch hit a single up the middle and tried to make it a double, but center fielder Jay Payton threw him out at second base. Umpire Robb Cook, however, ruled Knoblauch safe and cited Met first baseman Todd Zeile with obstruction for standing in the basepath. According to Cook, Knoblauch would have made it to second safely if he did not have to run around Zeile, so Cook awarded Knoblauch second base. Host manager Bobby Valentine was so upset that he tried to show the umpires the path Knoblauch took, and he was quickly ejected for inciting the crowd.

Knoblauch soon scored, and the Yankees led, 2–0, after the first inning. To find out how the game ended, read the next question.

CALL: In this play, common sense tells us that runners have the right to the basepaths when fielders are not involved in a play. Knoblauch should not have had to move even one step in order to avoid Zeile. He was delayed by the fraction of a second that may have cost him reaching second base safely, and the umpires disallowed the putout and awarded him second base.

The most confusing aspect to this play is the terminology, which is often misunderstood by players, managers, broadcasters, and newspaper reporters. When the defense gets in the way of a runner, it is called obstruction. When the offense gets in the way of a fielder, it is called interference. Confusingly, when the catcher gets in the way of a batter, it is also called interference, rather than obstruction.

7. **ANSWER:** The fielder has the right to field the ball. The runner is guilty of interference and is automatically out. If there had been fewer than two outs, and if the umpires had judged that

the runner interfered intentionally, then two outs would have been charged.

GAME: In the fourth inning of the same Yankees–Mets game as in the previous question, Todd Zeile was standing on first when Jay Payton hit a ground ball to Yankee second baseman Chuck Knoblauch. (Remember that in the first inning, Knoblauch had hit a ball to Payton and was obstructed by Zeile!) Perhaps Zeile was trying to take revenge on Knoblauch by running into him on the basepath. But this time, the umpires ruled interference and called Zeile automatically out.

Within the space of a few innings, Zeile had committed both obstruction and interference. The Yankees went on to win both games that day by identical scores of 4–2.

At the end of the 2000 season, the Yankees and Mets squared off again in the World Series. The result was the same, with the Bronx Bombers defeating their Queens rivals.

CALL: Obstruction and interference are easy to understand if you remember the following principles: When the defense is fielding a batted ball, the runners must get out of the way or risk being called out for interference; when the defense is not fielding the ball, the runners have full rights to the basepaths or they may become victims of obstruction.

These terms apply only to runners and fielders. When a batter is trying to hit, his action has the right of way over the catcher, who may be guilty of catcher's interference if his act of catching the pitch gets in the way of the swing. There are also rules that cover umpire's interference, in which the umpire hinders the defense (like when a batted ball hits an umpire or when the umpire blocks the catcher's attempted putout of a runner stealing a base).

8. **ANSWER:** Obstruction. He is awarded home base.

GAME: Proving the maxim that when it rains, it pours, there were no fewer than three highly unusual possible obstruction plays during a 2003 playoff game between the Oakland A's and Boston

Red Sox. This was one of the closest-fought playoff series in recent memory. Oakland had won the first game, 5–4, in 12 innings, after tying the score in the bottom of the ninth. The A's then won the second game, 5–1, and were on the verge of winning the best-of-five series when it moved to Boston for the third game.

With the score 0–0 in the bottom of the second inning of Game 3, two Oakland errors put Red Sox runners on first and third with one out. Then Damian Jackson hit a grounder to third baseman Eric Chavez, trapping teammate Jason Varitek in a rundown between third and home. A's catcher Ramon Hernandez chased Varitek almost all the way back to third, when Varitek ran into Chavez.

The umpires called obstruction on Chavez and awarded Varitek home base. This proved to be the Red Sox's only run until the 11th inning. In the meantime, there were two other controversial possible obstruction plays, both of which also went in the Red Sox's favor.

In the top of the sixth inning, the A's were threatening to score, with runners on first and third and one out. Miguel Tejada hit a ground ball to pitcher Derek Lowe, who tried to nab Oakland runner Eric Byrnes at home plate. Varitek, the Boston catcher, lunged for Lowe's poor throw, which flew past him and went all the way to the backstop. But in doing so, his body blocked the progress of Byrnes, who injured his ankle and started to limp back to the dugout under the misapprehension that he had touched the plate. In the collision, Byrnes missed the plate, and Varitek gathered the ball and tagged him out.

Because Varitek blocked Byrnes in the process of fielding the throw, it was not considered to be obstruction. Now there were two outs, and an intentional walk loaded the bases. The next batter was Hernandez, the Oakland catcher, who hit a ground ball that found its way past the glove of Red Sox shortstop Nomar Garciaparra for an error. Then lightning struck a third time.

Erubiel Durazo scored as Manny Ramirez got to the ball and fired it home. While rounding third base, Oakland runner

Tejada was obstructed by Boston's Bill Mueller. Upon hearing the obstruction call, Tejada all but stopped running and was tagged out by Varitek. The umpires ruled that Tejada would not have scored on the play, and so the out stood.

The score remained at 1–1 until the bottom of the 11th inning when pinch hitter Trot Nixon hit a game-ending two-run home run. The Red Sox went on to take the series with a dramatic come-from-behind 5–4 win in Game 4 and a 4–3 victory in the decisive fifth game. Their luck finally ran out, however, in the 11th inning of the seventh and final game of the American League Championship Series against the New York Yankees.

CALL: The penalty for obstruction depends on the circumstances surrounding it. If it occurs when a play is not being made on a player then the award is the base that the runner would have gotten had the obstruction not taken place. However, when a play is being made on a player, the penalty for the obstruction must be at least one additional base. When a play is not being made on a runner, it is a delayed dead ball. When a play is being made on a runner, the ball is dead immediately.

At first glance, this rule may seem unfair. In our example, Jason Varitek was running back to third base when he was obstructed, and yet he was awarded home and scored a run—a decisive run, as it happened. But the penalty is logical when you consider that awarding him third base would have been no penalty at all, since he had already obtained third base safely. When a runner is returning to a base, the defense would have almost nothing to lose by attempting to obstruct him, if the penalty did not involve the award of an additional base. The lesson here is that there is a strong disincentive to getting in the way of runners.

The other controversial calls in the A's–Red Sox playoff game illustrate further aspects of the obstruction rule. During the plateside collision between Varitek and Byrnes, both players had equal rights to be where they were—Varitek was fielding a thrown ball (not a batted ball, or else he would have had the right of way) and Byrnes was running the basepath—and so no obstruction or interference was called.

On the obstruction against Tejada, he was awarded third base (which he had not yet reached when Mueller got in his way). When he then slowed down, he effectively prevented the umpires from granting him home. Had he run his fastest and been thrown out by a whisker, then the umpires would probably have awarded the run. But when he stopped running, he removed his best argument that he could have made it home had the obstruction not taken place.

9. **ANSWER:** It is interference. The batter is also called out.
   GAME: The score was knotted 2–2, when the Chicago Cubs were attempting a rally against the host Philadelphia Phillies in 2003. With Jose Hernandez on third and Cub pitcher Carlos Zambrano standing on first, Mark Grudzielanek hit into this potential double play to end the half-inning. Instead of sliding toward second base, Zambrano slid toward Phillies shortstop Jimmy Rollins, whose throw would not have beaten Grudzielanek to first.

   This was ruled interference, and Grudzielanek was also called out, nullifying Hernandez's potential run home from third. This double play ended the threat and left the score tied at 2–2. Philadelphia went on to score 10 more times and won, 12–2.
   CALL: On an interference play like this, the umpires do not have to judge whether the interference was actually effective in preventing an out from being recorded. Other than obvious plays, such a call would be impossible to judge in any case, especially when the difference between out and safe is often measured in tiny fractions of a second. The penalty for interference is an out, regardless of what would have happened. Zambrano interfered with Rollins's attempt to put out Grudzielanek, and so Grudzielanek was called out.

10. **ANSWER:** Interference. The batter is out, and the runner returns to first.

GAME: Many baseball fans will recognize this play from the epic 2004 American League Championship Series between the Boston Red Sox and New York Yankees. The Yankees had won the first three games of the series, but then lost the next two.

In Game 6, the Yankees were trailing when Derek Jeter singled home a run to make the score Boston 4, New York 2. Then Alex Rodriguez hit a ground ball toward first base. Pitcher Bronson Arroyo gathered it up and tried to apply a tag when the ball came loose. Umpire Randy Marsh initially ruled Rodriguez safe, and it looked as though New York had made the score 4–3 with a runner in scoring position. But after Marsh conferred with the other umpires, who had a better view of the play, Rodriguez was called out for interference. The fan reaction was so violent that umpires had to clear the field, and there was a risk of the game being forfeited to the Red Sox. Order was restored, however, Jeter was sent back to first, and the game eventually ended as it was then, 4–2 to Boston. The Red Sox went on to win Game 7 and swept the World Series for their first championship since 1918.

CALL: Common sense tells us that runners do not have the right to slap the ball out of the hands or gloves of the defense. In these cases, the runner is out for interference, and no other runners can advance on the play. If the interference prevents a double play, then two outs would be charged.

The key to judging interference is the intent of the runner. In this example, Rodriguez clearly tried to knock the ball loose. Slapping at the ball is not a natural part of running to first base.

Often there will be a collision and a dropped ball during a play at the plate. When a runner trying to score collides with a catcher making a play on him and the catcher drops the ball, then the umpire must decide whether the collision was caused by the runner going home or by the runner going specifically for the ball. In plays at the plate, the umpire must also judge whether the catcher, before he gets the ball, intentionally blocks the path of the runner or is in the process of fielding the throw home. If he is blocking the plate without the ball, then he is obstructing the runner.

11. **ANSWER:** Yes, it was obstruction, and the runner should be awarded home plate.

    GAME: Clever infielders sometimes try to gain an unfair advantage by preventing runners from getting a clear view of a catch. In 2004, the clever infielder was Jose Lopez of the Seattle Mariners. Tino Martinez of the Tampa Bay Devil Rays flied out to Raul Ibanez in left field. Runner Carl Crawford broke for home, but then returned to third base.

    Umpire Paul Emmel called obstruction. Because Emmel felt that Crawford could have scored if he had had a better view of the catch, he awarded him home plate. This play ended the game, with the score Tampa Bay 2, Seattle 1.

    CALL: Obstruction is an act by the defense that impedes the progress of a runner. Normally, obstruction occurs when a fielder stands in the basepaths and blocks the route a runner is taking around the bases. But this play shows that obstruction can take other forms as well. The penalty is for the runners to be awarded the bases they would have reached if the obstruction had not occurred.

12. **ANSWER:** It is fan interference, and runners are awarded the bases that the umpires judge they would have attained had there been no interference. In this case, the batter was awarded a double and all three base runners were waved home to end the game.

    GAME: The Texas Rangers were trailing the visiting Chicago White Sox, 6–3, in the final frame of this nail-biter in 1991. With the help of an error, a walk, a hit batsman, and just one base hit, the Rangers had managed to claw back a run and load the bases. With two outs and the potential winning run on first, pinch hitter Monty Fariss came in to face Chicago reliever Bobby Thigpen. Rafael Palmiero was standing on third base, Reuben Sierra was on second, and Juan Gonzales was on first.

Fariss hit the ball hard into the corner, where it was touched by a fan. Third base umpire Joe Brinkman held his arms above his head and clasped his wrist to indicate fan interference. The three other umpires judged that if the fan had not interfered, then all three runners would have been able to score. This was the award they made, and the Rangers instantly won the game, 7–6. Many fans were left wondering what had happened because it is so unusual to see a runner—in this case Gonzales—awarded three bases during a dead ball situation.

13. **ANSWER:** Because it appeared as though the ball was over the fence when the fan reached for it, the play was ruled no interference—a home run. Replays later showed that the spectator had reached over the playing field, however, and the correct call should have been fan interference—in this case, an out.

    GAME: The Baltimore Orioles were visiting Yankee Stadium for the first game of the American League Championship Series in 1996. Neither team had won a World Series in more than a decade, and the level of excitement was high. Baltimore was ahead, 4–3, when New York's Derek Jeter hit a ball that looked as though it just might clear the short right field fence for a home run and draw the game even at 4–4.

    Baltimore's Tony Tarasco thought he had a good chance to make a catch when 12-year-old Jeffrey Maier wrote himself into baseball history. Umpire Rich Garcia ruled it a home run. Garcia later admitted that from a different angle, replays showed that the ball had not yet cleared the fence and Maier had stolen the ball from Tarasco. Because this was a judgment call, Oriole manager Davey Johnson had no grounds for appeal. The Yankees went on to win the game, 5–4, in extra innings thanks to a home run by Bernie Williams. They also won the ALCS and the World Series.

14. **ANSWER:** The ball was over the stands, giving the spectators the right to do as they pleased. This is not interference, so the play stood as a foul ball.

GAME: With plays like this one, it's no wonder that baseball fans are among the most superstitious people in the world. In 2003, the Chicago Cubs seemed on the verge of their first World Series appearance since 1945 when disaster struck.

Cub left fielder Moises Alou looked like he might catch Luis Castillo's foul pop, which drifted about one foot into the stands. Cub fan Steve Bartman, oblivious to Alou's presence, unwittingly robbed his team of a crucial out when he made contact with the ball. Umpire Mike Everitt ruled no interference because the ball was no longer over the playing field when Bartman touched it.

At this point, Chicago collapsed. After the non-catch, Castillo walked. Then there was a wild pitch, followed by a base hit. Shortstop Alex Gonzales committed only his 11th error all year when he dropped a routine ground ball that could have ended the half-inning. Before long, it was Marlins 8, Cubs 3, and Bartman had to be ushered out of the stadium. Florida also won the deciding seventh game of the championship series and went on to defeat the Yankees in the World Series.

CALL: The determining factor in fan interference is the location of the baseball. If the ball is on the playing field side of the wall, then the fielders have the right to make a play and any disruption by a spectator is interference. If the ball is on the spectator side, then the fans can go for the ball—or even go for the player—without the risk of interference.

In the interests of fairness, the rule on fan interference is that umpires impose whatever results would probably have transpired had the interference not taken place. This can be anything—an out, an advance by the runners, or perhaps just a foul ball. Fans in the first few rows must always be aware of the situation so that they do not hurt their team's chances when a live ball comes their way.

Chapter 4
Fielding

THE BALL GOES DEEP, AND . . .

Test your knowledge of plays and players that go deep into the outfield!

1. WHAT A MISPLAY!

Not all memorable plays and events are positive ones. In April, 1994, a Montreal Expos outfielder, normally a good one at that, once made the "Oops" blooper reels when he drifted into foul territory to haul in a Mike Piazza fly ball. Believing his catch was good for out number three, he handed the ball to a young fan in the first row of the stands and began to trot off the field.

Now, since there were actually only two men out, Los Angeles runner Jose Offerman alertly tagged up from first base. The outfielder, now realizing his folly, raced back to retrieve the ball. Eventually Offerman wound up at third base. Can you identify the fielder?

The answer is on page 91.

2. HELLO AND GOODBYE

In the sixth game of the 1947 World Series, this outfielder made a dazzling one-handed stab of a deep drive off the bat of Joe DiMaggio. It remains one of the most famous Series highlights ever. The outfielder lasted just four seasons in the majors and never gained much attention until his spotlight catch. Coincidentally, that defensive gem came in the final game of his career. Name this man.

The answer is on page 91.

3. TEAMS PLAYER

What outfielder, who has played for St. Louis, Atlanta, Los Angeles, and Texas, as well as for the Atlanta Falcons in the National Football League, when asked to describe the difference between baseball's spring training and pro-football's training camp replied, "One word. Pain!"

The answer is on page 91.

◆ ◆ ◆

GOING, GOING . . . HUH?

Can you determine if the ruling should be for a home run or not in the following situations?

4. OFF A FIELDER

As an outfielder tries to catch a long fly ball, he mistimes his jump and the ball bounces off his head and over the fence.

Is this a home run?

The answer is on page 91.

5. PINBALL

With a runner on first and no one out, the batter hits a deep fly ball to center field. The ball bounces off the top of the wall, rebounds back onto the forehead of a surprised centerfielder, and then ricochets over the fence.

Is this a home run?

The answer is on page 92.

6. CAUGHT

A batter hits a deep fly ball to right field. The right fielder leaps in the air and catches it, but his momentum carries him over the fence while in possession of the ball.

Is this a home run?

The answer is on page 92.

7. CAUGHT ON A RICOCHET

The batter hits a long fly ball to the warning track. The outfielder gets to it just in time, but bobbles the ball. Eventually, the ball rebounds off the fence and, without hitting the ground, is finally caught. This play is clearly not a home run, but it is useful to consider along with the other examples.

Is this a legal catch?

The answer is on page 92.

Chapter 4
ANSWERS

1. Larry Walker, winner of seven Gold Gloves. He later was able to shrug off his faux pas joking, "I get a lot of people asking me for balls now."

In a similar bonehead play from September 10, 1996, outfielder Derek Bell mistakenly lobbed a live ball into the stands. Clearly Bell thought the catch he made on a Marquis Grissom fly ball was the third out of the inning. A runner on first was awarded third on this miscue.

2. Al Gionfriddo.

3. Brian Jordan.

4. ANSWER: Home run.

GAME: The unlucky outfielder in this case was Jose Canseco, playing for the Texas Rangers in 1993. His outfield miscue gifted a home run to Cleveland Indian batter Carlos Martinez. Inevitably, the Indians won by a single run, 7–6. The blow seemed to have impaired Canseco's judgment because three days later he had the funny idea to pitch during a one-sided loss to the Boston Red Sox. Pitching a full inning soon led to elbow surgery, and the next year Canseco abandoned the outfield altogether and became a designated hitter. He was soon traded to the Red Sox, presumably not for his pitching or fielding abilities.

In a similar but less painful play in 2004, Philadelphia Phillies outfielder Jason Michaels was generous in helping a ball over the fence for a home run. Charles Thomas of the Atlanta Braves hit a deep fly ball that Michaels juggled twice before unintentionally flipping it into the hands of a spectator. Thomas's unexpected four-bagger did not affect the outcome of the game, which the Phillies won, 9–4.

5. ANSWER: Not a home run. A ground-rule double.

GAME: In this extremely rare and somewhat painful play in 1977, Warren Cromartie of the host Montreal Expos was at bat and Rick Monday of the Los Angeles Dodgers was the unlucky outfielder. When Monday deflected the ball into the crowd in fair territory, the umpires called a ground-rule double, sending runner Tony Perez to third and Cromartie to second. Perez soon scored the game-tying run in the Expos' come-from-behind 4–3 victory.

6. ANSWER: Not a home run. A legal catch.

GAME: Fenway Park in Boston has a very low fence between right field and the bullpen, and it has been the scene of a number of outfielders tumbling out of the playing field.

In 1997, Jay Buhner of the Seattle Mariners robbed Scott Hatteberg of the Boston Red Sox of a home run when he made a spectacular catch while falling over the outfield fence. The play, which made little difference in the Mariners' 4–0 loss, aggravated a bad knee, and Buhner soon had to have surgery.

In 2003, Bobby Kielty of the Toronto Blue Jays tumbled over the same fence when he caught a blast by Boston's Trot Nixon. The Red Sox scored plenty of runs in other ways that day and won, 9–4.

In both of these cases, there were no runners on base. But had there been base runners, then they would each have been awarded one base.

7. ANSWER: Not a catch.

GAME: In this incident in 1999, New York Yankee Derek Jeter was the batter and Baltimore Oriole Albert Belle was the ball-bobbling right fielder. Jeter wound up with a double that never touched the ground.

CALL: What is a home run? It seems an obvious question at first. A batted ball that flies over the fence without hitting the ground is a home run.

If the ball hits the ground before going over the fence, then it is a "ground-rule double" (not because it is a "ground rule" but because it is the rule for a ball that hits the ground; no stadium can create a "ground rule" that awards more or less than two bases on this play).

But what if the ball hits some combination of outfielder and outfield wall before going over? Here's where the rule gets interesting. The home run is governed by two separate rules, one for batters and one for runners. But first we need to understand some terms: A "bounding" ball is a ball that has hit the ground or the fence or something other than a defensive player; this contrasts with a ball "in flight" which has not hit anything, except possibly a fielder.

The rule that governs batters says that a home run is granted on a batted ball that goes over the fence without bouncing on the ground. The rule goes on to state that when a ball is deflected by a fielder over the fence in fair territory, it is a home run unless it is a bounding ball. This rule does not say anything about a bounding ball that goes over the fence without being deflected by a fielder. In contrast to this wording, the rule for runners states that a home run occurs when a ball goes over the fence in flight. Now let's apply these rules to our examples.

Martinez's blast that hit Canseco on the head was a home run by both rules. It was a home run for the runners because it was in flight. It was a home run for the batter because it was deflected by a fielder over the fence and it was not a bounding ball.

Javier Cromartie once blasted a ball that hit a fence before going into the croud, which is a ground-rule double by both rules. Because it hit the wall, it was no longer in flight, making it a double for the runners. And because it was a bounding ball that deflected off a fielder, it was a double for the batter.

Javier Valentin once hit a ball that hit windowsill on the fence before going over, and it was ruled a ground-rule double by the rule that governs runners because it was not in flight. But it seems to be a home run by the rule that governs batters because it did not bounce on the ground and was not deflected by a fielder.

In this case, the umpires ruled it a double, perhaps because the rule on batters does not specifically address this situation, while the rule on runners does. Also, the rule that covers runners is written in more general language and applies to batters as well, in their capacity as runners once they have hit the ball. In any case, it would be unthinkable to allow the batter to round the bases while only allowing the runners to advance two bases.

Now things get more confusing. Marquis Grissom of the San Francisco Giants had a game-winning hit off the top of the fence that is indistinguishable from Valentin's, at least according to the rulebook. It should have been a home run for the batter because it did not bounce on the ground and was not deflected by a fielder. But because it hit the fence before going over, it was not in flight, so it should have been a double for the runners. So why was this a home run, but Valentin's hit wasn't?

Here, common sense takes over where the rulebook lets us down. It seems that if a ball hits the top of the fence, then everything depends on where it goes next. If it goes over, then the umpires consider that in a sense it was already a home run when it stopped being in flight. If it comes back onto the field then it is not a home run.

But Valentin's hit also made it over the fence. Where, exactly, is the top of the fence for the purposes of this interpretation? The stadium design in Texas helped in this case, because the windowsill was clearly below a big yellow line on the fence. And, intuitively we can see why Valentin did not deserve a home run, while Grissom did. Of course, Martinez did not deserve a home run either, but Canseco's bone-headed play ensured that his hit was a home run.

Moving on, both Jay Buhner and Bobby Kielty made legal catches before leaving the field of play. Therefore, the outs counted even though they fell over the outfield wall.

I included Albert Belle's catch in order to illustrate the idea of a ball being "in flight." When a ball is no longer in flight, because it has hit the ground or a fence, then it can no longer be a home run and can no longer be caught for an out.

Are we clear so far? Here are some hypothetical situations that caused me to lose some sleep: What if an outfielder jumps to the top of the wall and reaches over to glove a ball that has deflected off the top of the wall and is headed into the crowd? Is it a home run already? Is it in flight? Is it a catch?

In all probability, this would be considered a base hit rather than a catch and the ball would remain in play. But it is no different from Grissom's home run, which must have been in flight by the logic of the home run rule that covers runners. If a ball is in flight, then it can be also caught for an out. How could Grissom's home run be in flight after it hit the top of the wall, but this hypothetical hit would no longer be in flight, just because a fielder was there to catch it?

Like in quantum mechanics, where subatomic particles can appear to be in two places at once, a hit off the top of the wall is simultaneously in flight and not in flight, and only settles into one or the other state of existence when it hits something else. If it continues into the crowd, then it is in flight and is a home run. If a fielder catches it, then it is not in flight and is not a catch.

Now, let's add a further twist. Let us say a fly ball bounces on the top of the fence and is continuing on its way over the fence, when an outfielder jumps up, grabs the ball in his glove, and falls into the crowd. Here we have a ball that is not in flight and therefore not caught for an out, but which is fielded by a player going into a dead ball area. My interpretation would be to treat this like an overthrow and award all runners two bases from the moment the outfielder falls over the wall. (It is not a one-base award, because that only applies to balls that are caught before the fielder falls out of play.)

Perhaps in addition to managers, each team should have a lawyer or a scientist in uniform in the dugout. Just try to remember that baseball is only a game, and, like backyard stickball, its rules must be updated to account for every unexpected situation that comes along.

Chapter 5

Catching

HARDER THAN IT LOOKS

Being the catcher isn't always as straightforward as it seems. Test your knowledge of famous catchers and infamous plays.

1. ODDITY

As the 1954 season wound down, Casey Stengel found himself in an unusual plight. His Yankees, normally the American League champs, had been eliminated from the pennant chase. Facing the Athletics, who were about to play their final game ever in Philadelphia, before the team was uprooted and moved to Kansas City, Stengel shook up his lineup. Bill "Moose" Skowron played second base instead of his normal first base position and center fielder Mickey Mantle handled shortstop duties, something he did seven times over his 18 years in the majors. Finally, Stengel's usual starting catcher played third for the only time in his 19-year career. Name that famous catcher.

The answer is on page 102.

2. QUICKIE

What catcher was flattened by a steamroller named Pete Rose when the all-time hit king scored the winning run in the 1970 All-Star game?

The answer is on page 102.

3. TOUGH ONE

In 1998, this Cincinnati catcher was astonished to discover the mammoth monetary demands Mike Piazza's agent had concocted when he negotiated a contract with Los Angeles. "I can't comprehend the money [said to be $100 million] Piazza is asking for. I can't comprehend the $80 million the Dodgers are offering. Heck, I can't comprehend what I'm making [$875,000]." Clues:

The speaker was once traded for Kenny Lofton; his first name is Eddie—who is he?

The answer is on page 102.

Here are some unusual plays involving catchers. Let's see if you can figure out the correct call.

4. A SWING AND A NICK

The bases are loaded with one out when the batter hits a ground ball to the pitcher. But on the swing, his bat nicks the catcher's mitt.

Because his swing touched the catcher's mitt, does the batter get another chance to hit?

The answer is on page 102.

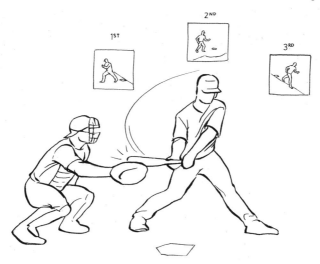

5. BEAN BALL

There is one out, a runner on first, and a full count on the batter. On the pitch, the runner takes off for second base. It is a swinging strikeout, and the catcher attempts to throw out

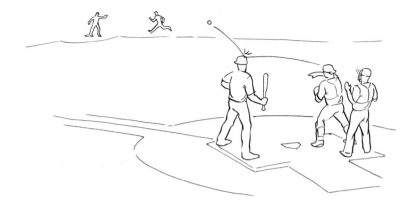

the runner going for second. On his throw, the catcher's arm nicks the umpire's facemask. When he releases the ball, it hits the batter in the head. The ball then bounces off the batter's helmet and into left field, and the runner reaches third base.

Does the runner get to stay on third, is he sent back to first, or is he out for possible interference by his teammate?

The answer is on page 103.

6. BIG SWING

With no outs and a runner on first base, the batter swings and misses for strike three as the runner tries to steal second. The

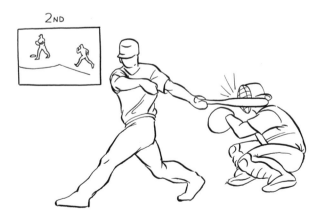

batter's backswing hits the catcher, who is unable to throw to second base to try to retire the runner.

Does the runner get to stay at second, is he sent back to first, or is he out for possible interference by his teammate?

The answer is on page 103.

7. UNMASKED

The score is tied in an extra-inning game, and the potential winning run for the home team is just 90 feet away on third base. The pitch comes in low, hitting the dirt. The batter swings and misses, and the ball bounces a few feet away from the catcher. Sensing a chance to win the game, the runner from third breaks for the plate. The catcher scoops up the ball with his mask and then applies the tag with the ball in his hand before the runner is able to score.

Is this a legal play by the catcher?

The answer is on page 104.

8. STRAY FOOT

The leadoff man for the visiting team begins a game with a base hit. The pitcher then gets two quick strikes on the next batter. Expecting a "waste pitch," the catcher lines up on the outside corner of the plate, with his foot slightly outside of the 43-inch catcher's box as the next pitch is delivered for a ball.

What is the penalty, if any, for the catcher's stray foot? What is the count?

The answer is on page 106.

Chapter 5
ANSWERS

1. Yogi Berra was Stengel's pick to play third that day. Many people forget, but Berra also played in the outfield in 260 contests. In fact, trivia experts recall the historic home run hit by Bill Mazeroski to clinch the 1960 World Series sailed over Berra in left field.

2. Cleveland Indians catcher Ray Fosse, in the bottom of the 12th inning. With two men out, Cincinnati's Rose singled and advanced to second on a base hit by Billy Grabarkewitz. Jim Hickman then singled, allowing the aggressive Rose to score when Amos Otis' throw from center field arrived a bit late to retire Rose at the plate.

3. Eddie Taubensee.

4. **ANSWER:** No. The batter is awarded first base.
   GAME: Playing in Cincinnati, the Milwaukee Brewers loaded the bases in the third inning of a scoreless contest in 2004. Pitcher Jimmy Haynes of the Reds thought he had pitched his way out of trouble when his offering to Craig Counsell came back to him for a possible double play to end the half-inning. But when Counsell's bat touched catcher Javier Valentin's mitt, it became a case of catcher's interference.

   Counsell was awarded first base, forcing home Wes Helms from third. This made the score 1–0. The Brewers' rally continued with an RBI single by Keith Ginter. Soon, Lyle Overbay hit a grand slam to make the score 6–0. The Brewers held on to win, 6–2, all thanks to the interference play that kept the Brewers' rally alive.
   CALL: Whenever the catcher's mitt touches a bat during a swing, it is catcher's interference. In most cases, the batter is awarded

first base. It is a delayed dead ball, so that if the batter gets a hit on the play and the other runners advance, then the play will proceed as if no interference took place. In some cases, the offensive manager may elect to decline the interference call. For example, if on a catcher's interference play the batter hits a sacrifice fly that scores a run, the batting team might prefer to keep the run and the out rather than have the batter go to first base and the other runner return to third.

5. **ANSWER:** It is umpire's interference, and the runner must return to first base.

   GAME: In 2005, the New York Yankees were visiting the Toronto Blue Jays when Blue Jay batter Frank Catalanotto struck out swinging. With Russ Adams stealing second, Catalanotto's momentum carried his head into the path of catcher Jorge Posada's throw, and the ball deflected into the outfield.

   Posada's arm, however, clipped the umpire, making it a case of umpire's interference. The ball was dead, and Adams was sent back to first base. The Yankees eventually won, 11–2.

6. **ANSWER:** It is a case of offensive interference in which no one is called out, and the runner must return to first base.

   GAME: The day after the Frank Catalanotto interference play, Russ Adams was again involved in this slightly different play, which had the identical result of preventing Jorge Posada's throw to second base. When striking out against Yankee relief pitcher Tom Gordon in the eighth inning, Adams' bat continued around and hit Posada on the backswing. Posada was unable to throw to second base on a steal attempt by Blue Jay Orlando Hudson. Hudson was returned to first base, but no outs were charged on this unintentional interference. The Yankees held on to win again, this time by the much slimmer margin of 4–3.

   Days after Posada was twice victimized by these interference plays, he committed catcher's interference when he got in the way of a swing by Darin Erstad of the newly christened Los

Angeles Angels of Anaheim. At one time, it seemed that where Posada went, interference followed.

CALL: The deflection off Catalanotto is fairly straightforward: The umpire interfered with the catcher's throw, and so the runner was returned to his original base. On the Adams strikeout, the same result applied because the interference happened on the backswing. Both plays bring up some intriguing possibilities had events unfolded slightly differently.

On either play, if Posada had been able to throw out the runner at second base despite the interference, then the out would still count on the assumption that it was not really interference after all. For this reason, it is a delayed dead ball.

The umpire's interference seemed to negate apparent batter's interference by Catalanotto. Had the umpire not gotten in the way and had Catalanotto intentionally interfered with the throw, then the runner would have been called out. What if Catalanotto had not struck out and intentionally interfered? In this case, the batter would be out and the runner sent back to his original base.

In a case of interference on a batter's backswing, as happened with Adams, then no out is charged and runners must return to their bases.

When the offense is guilty of interference, at least one person will be called out (except when the interference happens on the backswing). When the umpire causes interference, then no one is out.

7. **ANSWER:** No. It is an illegal use of equipment, and all base runners are awarded one base.

GAME: In this play, Mitch Webster of the Los Angeles Dodgers was batting against Jeff McCurry of the Pittsburgh Pirates in 1995, and the game was tied, 10–10. The game was truly remarkable, with 39 hits between both teams and yet no home runs. In the 10th inning, both sides had rallied for three runs, sending the marathon contest to the 11th. In the bottom of the 11th, when McCurry's pitch hit the dirt, rookie catcher

Angelo Encarnacion used his mask to grab the ball before he made the tag. The umpires ruled this to be an illegal use of equipment and awarded all base runners one base. This meant that instead of being out, the runner from third scored the winning run. Encarnacion was charged with the error that cost his team the game.

Encarnacion would probably like to forget this embarrassing moment from his brief Major League career. He made amends five days later, however, when he hit a rare inside-the-park home run in a victory over the Florida Marlins.

CALL: Part of the notion of fairness in baseball is that equipment should only be used for the purposes for which it is designed. Gloves and mitts are there to help players catch the ball. Masks protect catchers from being hit in the face. Hats are used to shade the eyes from the sun or stadium lights. The rule book specifies penalties for illegal use of equipment in order to prevent the defense from gaining an unfair advantage.

On a batted ball, if a defensive player takes off his hat to stop the ball or throws his glove to deflect the ball, the award is three bases—an automatic triple. This is one reason you never see outfielders throwing their gloves at balls they cannot reach. If a violation occurs (and equipment must actually touch the ball—there is no penalty for throwing a glove at the ball and missing), the ball remains alive, so the batter is able to try to score if he wants to risk it. If an outfielder throws his glove and stops a ball from passing over the fence for a home run, then the home run is awarded.

In the 1992 movie *A League of Their Own*, Madonna stars as center fielder Mae Mordabito, who tries to impress the crowd by catching a routine pop fly with her hat. If this were real baseball instead of a movie, then this play would not have been ruled an out, but would have been an automatic triple. (Hollywood take note: The author is available as a rules consultant for forthcoming movies, especially those starring female pop icons!)

On a thrown ball where a fielder commits a similar violation, the award is two bases. The rulebook does not actually mention pitched balls, however, which was what Encarnacion picked up with his mask. But the same logic applies. Here, the umpires reasoned by analogy with balls that go out of play: On a thrown ball that rolls out of play, the award is two bases; on a pitched ball that leaves the playing field, the award is one base. They concluded that illegal use of equipment on a pitched ball should also lead to a one-base award.

The umpires' quick thinking in this strange play shows that it is not enough for the men in blue to know the rule book. They need to understand the theory behind the rules, so that they can be prepared to make judgments on situations that may not yet be covered by the book.

8. **ANSWER:** It is a balk, and the runner is awarded second base. The count remains 0–2.

GAME: In the 2000 season, Ron Belliard of the Milwaukee Brewers got an infield single to start things off against Greg Maddux of the Atlanta Braves. With the count 0–2 against Marquis Grissom, rookie catcher Fernando Lunar placed his right foot outside the catcher's box. Umpire John Shulock called a balk and then ejected Braves manager Bobby Cox during the ensuing argument.

Belliard later scored on a fielder's choice, but he probably would not have done so if it weren't for the balk. A home run by Jeromy Burnitz in the fourth inning proved to be enough to give Milwaukee a 2–1 win, despite Maddux pitching a complete game.

Lunar later complained that the catcher's box seemed smaller that day. Controversially, the Braves' own television announcers argued that the team's groundskeepers had been painting the catcher's box too wide. Brewers manager Davey Lopes complained during the previous game, and the box seemed to shrink back down to regulation size for the game that Maddux started. If the catcher's box really was smaller that day, then no one told Lunar!

CALL: Catchers must position themselves with both feet in the catcher's box as pitches are delivered. The penalty for straying out of the box is a balk, meaning that all base runners get a free pass to the next base. This rarely happens, and when it does, it is usually during an intentional walk. The balk on Maddux's 0–2 pitch was an extremely rare example of this kind of play, and umpires have come to expect that an argument with the manager tends to follow rare events. Manager Bobby Cox would hesitate, however, to blame the umpires for another rare event that happened that day: Burnitz's 454-foot home run was the longest in the history of Turner Field at that time.

Chapter 6

Umpping

THE ORIGINAL "MEN IN BLACK"

Umpires were once nicknamed "the men in black" when their uniforms were still traditionally that color. Fashion aside, it's your turn to "witness" situations and make a split-second call.

1. GROUND RULE

Moises Alou was playing left field in Wrigley Field for the Cubs. Houston's Adam Everett ripped a ball that deflected off Alou's glove and nestled in the ivy on the wall. Alou hoisted his arms giving the usual signal to umpires that a ball was lost, not in play. What ruling did the umps make?

The answer is on page 120.

2. INFIELD FLY SITUATION

When Orlando Gomez was Tampa Bay's bullpen coach, he discussed a bizarre play he once saw involving the infield fly rule in a bases-loaded situation. The batter lofted a high fly to the infield and was, of course, by the nature of the rule, declared out. However, the ball got lost in the sun, fell to the dirt, and skipped a short distance away from the nearest fielder. The runner off third took off for home, and an ensuing throw came home also, but "the catcher forgot to tag the guy; he forced the runner by tagging home plate instead of the runner."

In this situation would you call a double play, render the ball dead and send the runner back to third, allow the run to score, or scratch your head in puzzlement?

The answer is on page 120.

3. GIVE HIM THE THUMB

Can an umpire eject a batter from a game during an intentional walk?

The answer is on page 120.

4. YOU'RE BLIND, UMP

An organist playing at a minor league park in 1993 decided to play "Three Blind Mice" as that day's umpires took to the field just prior to the game. Witty, perhaps, but it was offensive to the umpiring crew.

One year prior to that, Jerry Burkot, the public address announcer for another minor league team, the Greensboro Hornets, also ruffled some egos. After what he felt was a questionable third strike call, he piped the theme song from "The Twilight Zone" over the sound system. Earlier he had been warned not to play that tune to mock the umps, but he couldn't resist.

Do umpires have the right to eject teams' personnel such as the men mentioned, or do their "veto" powers of thumbing someone apply only to players, managers, and coaches?

The answer is on page 120.

5. FINAL EJECTION SCENARIO

The Morning Journal featured an odd tale that took place when Detroit hosted Cleveland on May 2, 1995, in a contest being umpired by a crew of replacements who were hired due to a labor dispute involving big league umps. Positive that the pitch he delivered to Tigers outfielder Bobby Higginson was a strike, Dennis Martinez stormed off the mound. He confronted home plate umpire Gus Klein, holding the ball directly over the middle of home plate, indicating where the pitch had traveled. Is this case of "showing up the umpire" enough to get Martinez tossed?

The answer is on page 121.

6. SWITCH PITCH

Switch-hitters are common in professional baseball, but pitchers who have the skill to throw with both arms are as rare as sweet talk between Yankees and Red Sox.

During his high school days, Paul Richards once won the first game of a doubleheader while throwing righty then came back to win the nightcap while firing the ball lefty. In a minor league contest Richards, normally a right-hander, was on the mound when a pinch-hitter strolled to the plate. It was Charlie Wilson, a switch hitter.

Question: As an umpire, what would you do in this situation? Wilson took his position to bat left-handed against Richards, but when he did so Richards simply took the glove off his left hand, switched the ball to that hand, and was prepared to go at Wilson lefty-on-lefty, an advantage for the pitcher. Can Wilson now turn around and decide he's going to bat righty after all? Could Richards then change his mind again? What's your call?

The answer is on page 121.

7. HOW MANY OUTS?

It doesn't happen often, but players are human and do forget the number of outs sometimes. In 1979, Joe Ferguson was batting for the Dodgers against the Pittsburgh Pirates with the bases loaded and a payoff pitch on the way. Lee Lacy, the runner off third, saw what he believed was strike three, but was actually ball four. Unaware, Lacy trudged toward the dugout.

Confusion set in when Pirates catcher Manny Sanguillen also thought the inning was over! He removed the ball from his mitt and rolled it toward the mound for the start of the next inning. At that point Jim Wynn, the runner from second base, sprinted around third and crossed home plate. Lacy finally snapped out of his confusion and streaked across the plate, too. After unraveling the mess, the umpires made a ruling—what was it?

The answer is on page 121.

8. TIME OUT NEEDED!

A game on August 29, 1992, featured a huge mental mistake. Pitcher Charlie Leibrandt racked up his 1,000th career strikeout. Wishing to save the souvenir ball, he gently bowled it into his team's dugout. Big problem—he had failed to call a time out. Is the ball alive? Could the only base runner at the time, Ricky Jordan, advance?

The answer is on page 122.

9. INTERFERENCE VERSUS OBSTRUCTION

On August 6, 2004, Carl Crawford of the host Tampa Bay Devil Rays was on third base with the bases loaded and one out in the 10th inning of a 1–1 contest. Tino Martinez raised a fly ball to left field causing Crawford to head back toward third in order to tag up. Seattle's shortstop, Jose Lopez, purposely placed himself in a position to block Crawford's view of the catch by outfielder Raul Ibanez, hoping Lopez wouldn't get a good jump in his effort to score. What ruling would you make here?

The answer is on page 122.

10. REVERSAL

On July 28, 2004, Justin Morneau of the Minnesota Twins hit a long drive that was ruled a homer by umpire Ed Montague. Chicago White Sox manager Carlos Guillen and his left fielder Carlos Lee protested the call. Replays revealed that the ball had hit the top of the fence and had ricocheted back onto the field. Can the umpiring crew reverse such a call?

The answer is on page 122.

11. TOUCH 'EM ALL

It was the bottom of the 15th inning of the fifth game of the 1999 National League Championship Series. The bases were full of Mets and Atlanta's rookie pitcher Kevin McGlinchy had his work cut out, facing veteran Robin Ventura in a 3–3 tie.

Ventura won the confrontation, belting a grand slam, a dramatic blow, on the 482nd pitch of the five hour and forty-six-minute game. Hold on, though. Ventura touched first base just moments before a wild and jubilant celebration broke out. Mobbed by teammates, he never bothered to run around the base paths. What's your call here?

The answer is on page 122.

12. SIMILAR PLAY

When Chris Chambliss hit the pennant-winning, ninth-inning walk-off homer for the Yankees versus Kansas City in the 1976 American League Championship Series, things were a bit different. He glided around the bases until a throng of fans engulfed him at home plate. It was unclear if he had touched the plate or not.

As a matter of fact, about an hour after the game he returned to the field to step on home plate, just in case he had missed it. Alan Robinson of the AP quoted Chambliss as saying, "Home plate was gone. Somebody had already taken it. There were no umps there, either." In theory, could Kansas City have appealed the play later?

The answer is on page 123.

13. IT USUALLY PAYS TO STEAL

Roger Cedeno stole third base for the Mets on a play in which home plate ump Sam Holbrook got in the way of Yankees catcher Jorge Posada, who was trying to unleash a throw. Is it Posada's responsibility to get into a position to get his throw off, or is the umpire at fault here?

The answer is on page 123.

14. GOING AGAINST THE GRAIN

Is there anything in the rule book that prohibits a switch-hitter who is, say, facing a left-handed pitcher, from batting lefty? Obviously, this would be poor strategy on the surface of things, but if you were the umpire would you allow this?

The answer is on page 123.

15. RUNNER AND BALL MEET

A base runner off first base is headed toward second on a grounder. Suddenly, the ball strikes him on an erratic hop. As the ump, what ruling do you make?

The answer is on page 124.

16. STAYING INSIDE THE LINES

Let's say Craig Biggio of the Houston Astros is dashing down the

line, trying to beat out a grounder. He's safe on a photo finish at first, but he did not stay inside the "lane," the restraining path that's delineated by chalk near the first-base bag. In running outside that lane, he made contact with the first baseman. Is the contact incidental, or is Biggio violating a rule?

The answer is on page 124.

17. WILD TIMES

During the fourth game of the American League Championship Series of 1999, things got rather wild. In the bottom of the ninth, frustrated Boston Red Sox fans threw bottles on the field, resulting in an eight-minute delay. New York Yankees players, at risk, were hustled off the field. Yankees second baseman Chuck Knoblauch commented, "That's not a safe situation. You have to have eyes all over the place." Can an umpire in this situation stop the game entirely?

The answer is on page 124.

18. WRONG CALL

The Houston Astros met the St. Louis Cardinals on April 24, 2005, and, in the sixth inning, loaded the bases to set up a bizarre event. Cards third baseman Scott Rolen made a back-handed stab on a short hop line drive off the bat of Craig Biggio. Rolen stabbed the bag with his spikes for a force out and rifled the ball across the infield to nab Biggio. Then, when first baseman Albert Pujols applied a tag to Willy Taveras, who was still standing on the bag at first, the ump called Taveras out for the completion of a triple play. Just one problem, though: It isn't a triple killing—why not?

The answer is on page 124.

19. EJECTION TIME FOR THE EARL OF BALTIMORE

Baltimore manager Earl Weaver was notorious for his volatile temper and for the numerous ejections that resulted from his ire. One day, veteran umpire Tom Haller spotted Weaver smoking a cigarette in the dugout during a game; he immediately gave Weaver the boot.

The next day the impish Weaver strolled to home plate to present his lineup card to the umpiring crew prior to the game. Haller once more spotted a cigarette in Weaver's mouth and ejected him again. Instead of getting upset, Weaver grinned and displayed his candy cigarette to Haller. Not amused, Haller kicked him out of the game before a single pitch was thrown. Is this a legitimate call?

The answer is on page 125.

20. POST GAME BLUES

It's May 7, 1997, and umpire Dale Ford's out call on Scott Brosius has just ended a 1–0 nailbiter. Brosius, upset that he was out at the plate and that his Oakland A's lost on that close call, fired his helmet to the turf and screamed at Ford. When A's manager Art Howe unleashed another tirade against Ford, he, too, was kicked out.

But can a man get kicked out of a game that's over?

The answer is on page 125.

21. GUARANTEED NIGHT OFF

One veteran ump said there are three things he would not permit a manager, coach, or player to do. Violating these three rules meant instant ejection. Can you name two?

The answer is on page 125.

22. FAUX PAS

Astrologists would love the wacky events of September 9, 1999, which numerically works out to 9–9–99. The San Diego Padres played host to the Montreal Expos in a game they'd go on to win, 10–3. In the seventh inning, the stars were aligned in favor of the Padres for a while. Reggie Sanders of the Padres struck out for the inning's third out, but nobody—not the umps, the Padres, or the Expos—realized the inning was over. That brought Phil Nevin to the plate. He worked the count to 2 and 1 against Ted Lilly before a member of the Expos called the mistake to the attention of home plate ump Jerry Layne. What happened next?

The answer is on page 125.

23. THE CALL TO THE PEN

Freddy Garcia was on the mound for Ozzie Guillen's Chicago White Sox on July 22, 2004, facing the Indians. He was coasting along into the eighth inning with nine strikeouts racked up. However, when he walked leadoff hitter Omar Vizquel, Guillen, who had a lefty and a righty warming up in the bullpen, felt it was time to make a change. As Guillen marched to the mound to lift Garcia, he knew he wanted southpaw Damaso Marte to enter the game. However, he inadvertently motioned with his right hand to indicate he wanted rightly reliever Cliff Politte to replace Garcia. If you were the umpire, what would you do here?

The answer is on page 125.

24. HE THREW HIS WHAT?!

A strange, seldom-called rule came into play during a Los Angeles versus Arizona contest on May 28, 2005. Dodgers reliever, hard-throwing Duaner Sanchez, faced Luis Terrero, who hit a soft line drive that was headed back through the box. At first Sanchez leaped for the ball as if to stab it with his glove in the orthodox manner, but when he realized the ball was too high to haul in, he quickly removed his mitt from his left hand and tossed it right-handed at the ball. Further, he hit the ball in flight! He then scrambled over toward the earthbound ball, recovered it, and shoveled it to first base, a bit late to retire Terrero. If you had been the umpire that day, what would your ruling have been on this offbeat play?

The answer is on page 126.

25. INFIELD FLY PUZZLE

A strange play occurred on September 3, 2004 in Tampa. Detriot's Craig Monroe doubled to start an inning and Carlos Pena followed, drawing a walk. Marcus Thames then popped one up to Devil Rays shortstop Julio Lugo, who apparently lost the ball in the domed roof. The ball fell harmlessly to the ground. Monroe took off for third and Pena moved to second, but not before a Tampa fielder stepped on third base. What's the correct call to clarify this mess?

The answer is on page 126.

26. SCORER'S DECISION

Put away your umpire's equipment and pretend you're the scorer at a baseball game. How would you rule this play? On June 27, 2005, Boston's Trot Nixon, in a play similar to one made famous by Jose Canseco, was crestfallen when a long drive off the bat of Cleveland's Grady Sizemore deflected off his glove and into the stands, just a few yards to the left of the 380' marker in right field. Nixon had backpedaled on the ball, got turned around a bit, and although he did get the tip of his mitt on the ball, it set to rest in the visitor's bullpen. That turned a 4–0 Cleveland lead into a 6–0 cushion in the seventh inning.

Incidentally, in Canseco's more embarrassing incident, also against the Indians, the fly ball hit off his head and over the wall! Meanwhile, is Nixon charged with an error or do you award a homer to Sizemore?

The answer is on page 126.

27. HE SHOULDA SLID

The scene was set: Game 5 of the 1968 Fall Classic between St. Louis and Detroit, with the Cards holding a commanding three-games-to-one lead. Cardinals ace Bob Gibson, with his phenomenal 1.12 ERA, had squared off twice against 31-game winner Denny McLain and had won both times, putting St. Louis in a pretty spot. Up by a run in the fifth inning, Cardinals speed merchant Lou Brock doubled, representing an insurance run. Julian Javier then singled to left where Willie Horton fielded the ball. Brock "nonchalanted" his way home, never sliding even though doing so could have resulted in a bang-bang play at the plate. He was tagged out.

Home plate ump Doug Harvey later mused, "He crossed home plate without touching it. He came in standing up. He should have slid."

In the long run, did it matter or not—who won that Series?

The answer is on page 126.

Chapter 6
ANSWERS

1. Normally when a ball is, say, lodged under a fence or hidden among vines, the batter is awarded a ground rule double. However, once Alou touched the ball, that ground rule is not in effect. Everett was free to circle the bases, which he did. The scorer ruled the play a double and a two-base error. After the game Alou meekly told the gathered media, "I didn't know the rule." He added jokingly, "That's why I can't manage when I retire."

2. Orlando Gomez said, "There's no force, you have to tag the guy to make the double play." Therefore, since the rule states the ball is live and runners can advance at their own risk, the run stands. The force play no longer existed once the batter was automatically ruled out in this infield fly scenario.

3. An umpire can kick a player out of a game at any time, but it's hard to imagine a batter who is about to get a free pass to first being angry enough to do anything to precipitate an ejection. Yet it has happened. Terry Francona, who would go on to manage the Red Sox to world championships in 2004 and 2007, once was tossed from a game immediately after drawing an intentional walk. With bad blood already existing between him and home plate ump Ken Kaiser, Francona fumed when Kaiser muttered, "Can you believe they're intentionally walking you?" Having been insulted, Francona snapped, and accused the umpire of not hustling on an earlier play. Moments later, after ball four had been lobbed, Kaiser gave him the thumb in an odd baseball moment.

4. In both cases, the offending parties were kicked out of the game. In Burkot's instance, he was escorted out of the building on orders from an umpire. Sheriff's deputies took him away in handcuffs according to reports.

5. Normally, yes. Umps will allow a player to grumble about a call, but once a player shows an entire stadium that he is questioning the umpire's authority, such behavior results in the ol' heave-ho.

In this circumstance, with an umpire who was perhaps intimidated by his surroundings, he let the Martinez tirade pass. Tigers manager Sparky Anderson observed, "In 26 years I've never seen a pitcher go to the plate and hold the ball over the plate. The umpire said he should have thrown him out of the game, but by the time he realized it, it was too late."

Martinez was also responsible for another rarity that day— he apologized to Klein and confided that he "should have thrown me out. He just smiled." Martinez also pointed out that if a "real" umpire had been working the game, "I'd be back in Cleveland now. But if we had a real ump, he wouldn't have missed the call."

6. The rule now states that the batter gets the final say in determining the match-up. It also indicates a pitcher can change hands on every pitch if he desires to do so. He is required to make his decision concerning which arm to use before stepping on the mound so the batter can then choose which batter's box he wants to enter.

However, in the Wilson vs. Richards case, records show Richards played it coy. He put both of his feet on the rubber, hid the ball behind his back, cradling it with both hands, and waited for Wilson to make his final decision as to which way he'd hit. At that point, Richards began his delivery throwing with the arm that gave him an edge over Wilson. Nevertheless, the result wound up in Wilson's favor when, quite anticlimactically, Richards walked him.

7. The pitch had been called ball four so the walk was issued to Ferguson. More important, since the ball was live, Lacy's run counted, but Wynn was ruled out for passing a runner and the inning of insanity was finally over.

In a not-as-messy situation from August 4, 1996, White Sox catcher Robert Machado rolled the ball back to the mound after a strikeout. He and pitcher Jim Parque were certain they had retired the side and began to leave the field. On the other hand, the alert Fred McGriff of Tampa Bay realized there were only two men out and scored all the way from second.

8. With no time out, the ball was alive, naturally. The runner advanced to second on this blunder.

9. Lopez is guilty of obstruction and gets charged with an error. Crawford was allowed to score the winning run and the game was over.

10. The umpiring crew can and they did, changing the call from a homer to a double. Interestingly, later in that game Morneau drove a ball deep down the line in right that was ruled a home run by umpire Matt Hollowell. However, after another White Sox gripe, the umps huddled to be sure the correct call had been made, and once again they changed their decision. Not at all surprisingly, indignant Minnesota manager Ron Gardenhire, feeling ripped off, argued vehemently and was eventually ejected from the game.

11. The Mets still won since the runner from third base did touch home and Ventura did reach first base safely. Ventura robbed himself of a home run, though, and the final score was decreed to be 4–3 on Ventura's 300-plus foot single; one writer called it a "grand slam-single."

    Steve Hirdt, a spokesman for the Elias Sports Bureau, explained to the AP, "The game ends in sudden death when the winning run scores. The only exception is on a home run, assuming the player rounds all the bases. He never rounded the bases." Ventura noted, "I saw it go over and then I just ran to first. As long as I touched first, we won. So that's fine with me."

12. No. First of all, an appeal or, for that matter, a request to play a game under protest would have had to have been made before the team left the field. Secondly, as Chambliss remembered, "A few of them [umpires] told me years later that the run counted because it was the fans that were in the way." In other words, it wasn't Chambliss' fault that he couldn't reach home plate under such unusual circumstances.

13. During that game, part of an interleague "Subway Series" in July 1999, Holbrook ruled himself guilty of interference and Cedeno had to return to second.

14. Of course the hitter may bat from either side of the plate. Yes, this happens occasionally when a switch-hitter has had a history of frustration and failure against a given pitcher. For instance, in the third game in the 1999 Division Series between the Atlanta Braves and the Houston Astros, Carl Everett, a switch-hitting outfielder who had great numbers in the regular season (.325, 25 hr, 108 runs driven in) went up against Atlanta lefty Tom Glavine, a Cy Young Award winner. Everett had been stymied to the tune of 1 for 12 lifetime against the tough pitcher so he figured, "What the heck, I'll try batting left-handed against him."

In the first inning, he drew a walk. In his next at bat, he reached on an infield hit, beating the throw to first by about one stride, after he had slapped the ball to second baseman Bret Boone, who had to backhand the ball. Assuming that Everett would have hit the ball in the same location, and assuming Boone would have been playing him the same way defensively had Everett been hitting the ball right-handed, Everett would not have beat the ball out. When a player bats left-handed, he is at least a step closer to first base since he begins in the batter's box nearer to first and that can make a difference on many a close play.

For the record, in his third at-bat Everett fanned against Glavine and in the bottom of the 10th inning he came to the plate against another lefty, John Rocker, with the bases loaded. It was a situation in which even a fly ball hit deeply enough for a sacrifice fly would have won the game. This time, relieved that he was not facing his nemesis Glavine, Everett turned around and batted righty, but made a harmless out.

All of this illustrates a point—hitters will make changes, even rather drastic ones, if they believe such actions may improve their chances of success.

15. Under normal conditions, such as with the infield not playing in, the ball is ruled dead, and the runner is out, but the batter is credited with a hit and is awarded first base. Houston Astros star Craig Biggio once joked, "That's a great team rule because if a guy's struggling and you're [as the runner] going to be out anyway, you might as well kick the ball for the guy so he can get a hit." He laughed and said that while that could happen, it's almost always unintentional.

16. Actually, if the umpire feels Biggio interfered with the play regardless of where he is, he would definitely be ruled out. Biggio had no problem with the interference aspect of the rule, but he felt the placement of the path to be a foolish baseball decision. "Why is that [restraining path] line running down the side of the first base line in foul territory when the base is in fair? So you gotta run [in foul territory] and step in fair; that's pretty stupid."

17. He cannot only end the game, he can forfeit it as well. In this case, matters didn't get that extreme and no ump wants to forfeit any contest, let alone a playoff contest. The Yankees had led by a single run entering the ninth, then went on a binge which upset the Fenway spectators, and cruised to a 9–2 victory. Things got so tense and dicey in this rivalry, Yankees wives had to be escorted from the park by police.

18. The first-base ump thought Rolen had snared Biggio's line drive in the air. Basing his ruling on that, he made the correct call. However, when the umps huddled and discussed the play, they sorted things out: It is a double play and Taveras, not forced to leave his base once Biggio was retired, is safe.

19. Yes. The umpires have a whole lot of clout and Weaver's ejection stood. On June 6, 1986, San Diego Padres skipper Steve Boros also was thumbed before the game began. When he met with the umpires pre-game, he tried to hand umpire Charlie Williams a videotape of a play Boros thought Williams had blown the night before. Williams quickly let it be known he would not tolerate such antics.

20. Yes, a man can get kicked out of a game that's over. Ford explained, "You write it up [in an official report] as an ejection, then the league president can do what he wants to do about it."

21. The ump said he would not tolerate "direct profanity [aimed at him]," nor would he allow anyone to "get personal, or delay the game."

22. The mistake must be corrected immediately. The inning is over and Nevin's at-bat is wiped out.

23. In real life the crew chief, Joe West, politely listened to Guillen's plea, but insisted he must bring Politte in. "I screwed up," Guillen admitted. "I told the umpire, 'OK, bring in whoever you want.' It turned out that umpire helped us win the game." Actually, it was the fine pitching of Politte that did the trick. Although left-handed hitters carried a proud .357 batting average to the plate against him, on that day he put out the fire, eventually ending the threat by inducing a double play.

    Guillen later joked, "The next time I go out there, I'm going to raise both arms and see who the umpires bring out."

24. The correct rulebook call is to award an automatic triple to Terrero, meaning Sanchez's throw and Terrero's dash to the bag had been moot. Some observers assumed Sanchez was not aware of this rare rule, but he confessed he did know of it but made the misplay because he simply got caught up in the action. Sadly for Dodger fans, they had been winning prior to this rare triple but went on to drop the decision to the D-backs. In fact, later in the same inning Sanchez got hurt when he served up a homer to opposing pitcher Javier Vasquez, his first big league homer ever.

25. Thames is out, of course, on the infield fly rule. Monroe and Pena were permitted to advance at their own risk (or, of course, they could have safely stayed at second and first, respectively). When the defense retrieved the ball, but failed to tag either runner, the base runners were ruled safe and remained on second and third since there was no force play once Thames was automatically ruled out.

After the game, Tigers manager Alan Trammell confessed, "We were very fortunate, I'm not going to lie to you. It could have been a triple play, but it worked out in our favor."

26. The play was ruled a home run. ESPN analyst John Kruk, a former outfielder (and first baseman), felt the ruling should have been a four-base error. The Fenway Park official scorer disagreed, feeling it wasn't "a routine play" for the outfielder. Nixon's frustration after the ball nestled into the bullpen seems to have indicated he believed it was a play he needed to and/or could have made.

27. It mattered. From that point on, the Tigers stormed back and won it all in a seven-game set.

Chapter 7
Managing and Coaching

HERE'S YOUR CHANCE TO PULL THE STRINGS AND CALL THE SHOTS

Put yourself in the mind of managers and coaches to make the calls that really matter.

1. STRANGE MOVE

Your name is Lloyd McClendon and you are the manager of the 2004 Pittsburgh Pirates. It's August 11 and you're facing the San Francisco Giants. The game is tied in the 10th inning and Barry Bonds, who once launched 73 home runs in a season, steps to the plate to get things started. In this situation, would you consider issuing a leadoff intentional walk?

The answer is on page 142.

2. ANOTHER STRANGE MOVE

During a game in which Walt Alston managed the Brooklyn Dodgers, hard-hitting Roy Campanella was batting with the runner off first base representing the game-winning run. There were two outs and a 3-and-1 count, so Campanella was expecting to see a good pitch to whack at. However, Alston had his third-base coach flash the "take" sign. Seconds later, quite dismayed at having just seen a juicy fastball go by for a called strike, taking him to a full count, Campanella dug in again, puzzled by the decision to take a pitch. What was Alston's logic behind this seemingly strange maneuver? If you were running the Dodgers, would you have made that call?

The answer is on page 142.

3. BACK TO BONDS

The San Francisco Giants took on Randy Johnson and his Arizona Diamondbacks on July 9, 2004. With San Francisco runners on first and second in the bottom of the fifth, the game, then tied at three apiece, had reached a crucial moment. A classic confrontation arose: Johnson with his 4,000-plus strikeouts versus the much-feared Bonds in a lefty-on-lefty match-up featuring future Hall of Famers. Normally, Johnson would not walk a batter in this situation, but would you direct him to give four wide ones to Bonds?

The answer is on page 143.

4. PLAYING IT BY THE BOOK

In baseball jargon, playing it "by the book" refers to managerial decisions that make the most sense percentage-wise, conforming totally to analytical scouting reports and computer printouts. Sometimes a manager will play it by the book and other times he'll make decisions based more on his heart and gut instinct.

Imagine you are Phil Garner when he led the Milwaukee Brewers back in 1999. Southpaw Jesse Orosco, an outstanding reliever, is in your bullpen anxiously waiting to enter the game, but a pack of right-handed hitters are due up. Would you consider making the call to Orosco anyway?

The answer is on page 143.

5. GOING AGAINST CONVENTIONAL THINKING

Yet another example of going against the book took place during the 2004 American League Championship Series. Joe Torre, the New York Yankees skipper, told the press later that when his team played the Boston Red Sox in cozy Fenway Park, its dimensions caused him to sometimes alter his thinking process regarding stolen base attempts with runners in scoring position. How could the stadium's size and configuration influence his strategy in this regard?

The answer is on page 143.

6. THROW THE BOOK AWAY?

During the 1999 season, Tony Muser, the manager of the Kansas City Royals, was faced with a dilemma with his team playing the Texas Rangers. The Rangers had a runner on second courtesy of a sacrifice bunt, and Rusty Greer coming to the plate. He would be followed by Juan Gonzalez, a master at knocking in runs. First base was open, but the Royals needed a double play. Did Muser elect to pitch to Greer, or did he walk him to set up a double play? Had this been your call, what would you have done?

The answer is on page 144.

7. CALL TO THE BULLPEN?

In July 1999, Detroit Tigers manager Larry Parrish said, "We've been using the [computer and scouting] matchups of how some guys do against our pitchers to help decide which reliever to bring in, and we've been beat a couple times by pitchers who never gave up a hit to this guy—but you bring him in to pitch and, boom, base hit and game's over."

With that string of bad luck against Parrish, what did he do when his Tigers squared off against the Cincinnati Reds in a key spot with the dangerous Greg Vaughn at the plate? The situation was this: Vaughn, who wound up the season with 45 homers, was a good candidate to hurt Detroit with his stick or, on the other hand, to strike out—he ended the year with a staggering 137 whiffs.

Parrish had Willie Blair up in the bullpen, but, as Parrish recalled, "At the time, he was like 8-for-12 off Willie with a couple of homers." Did Parrish play it the conventional way, relying on printouts, and go to the pen for a pitcher who had a history of doing well versus Vaughn, or did he elect to chance it with Blair?

The answer is on page 144.

8. HARGROVE TOOK A CHANCE

Then there was an incident that took place on August 18, 1999. The Cleveland Indians were playing the Rangers and the blazing hot Rafael Palmeiro came to the plate in the seventh inning. The score was tied at one run each, with Rangers dancing off second and third. An obvious call would be to order an intentional walk from right-handed pitcher Charles Nagy to the left-handed hitting Palmeiro. Was this another situation where the manager Mike Hargrove didn't make the "normal" move?

The answer is on page 144.

9. PLAYING THE LEFTY-LEFTY PERCENTAGES

It's June 28, 2005, and the Los Angeles Angels and Texas Rangers, the two top dogs in the American League West Division, are battling in an early showdown. Knotted at one run apiece and entering the 11th inning, the Angels load the bases with star outfielder Garret Anderson coming to the plate. If you were in the trembling spikes of Texas manager Bucky Showalter, do you go to the pen to bring a southpaw into the game to face the left-handed hitting Anderson?

The answer is on page 145.

10. CHECK AND DOUBLE-CHECK

This time you play the role of Buddy Bell, managing the Kansas City Royals in 2005 after replacing Tony Pena. On July 1, you turn in your lineup card to the umpires prior to the game's first pitch against the visiting Angels. In the bottom of the first inning, David DeJesus gets your Royals off to a fine start by banging a single. That brings Angel Berroa to the plate.

But wait—the umpires huddle and point out that, according to the card presented to them, Berroa is hitting out of order;

Berroa is supposed to hit leadoff and DeJesus is penciled in as the number two man in the batting order.

Two questions: When the umps rule DeJesus must abandon his berth on first and bat again with an automatic out being declared on Berroa's spot in the lineup, do you protest this call, or are they correct? Secondly, who is responsible for the botched lineup card—one of your coaches or yourself?

The answer is on page 145.

11. AN OLDER MOVE

In Game 4 of the 1947 World Series between the Yankees and the Dodgers, New York hurler Bill Bevins was flirting with history, carrying a no-hitter into the ninth inning. With one out and nursing a one-run lead, Bevins walked Brooklyn's Carl Furillo and then got the next batter on a pop-up. Al Gionfriddo swiped second as a pinch runner, putting the tying run in scoring position.

At that point pinch hitter Pete Reiser, a pretty dangerous stick coming off a .309 season, was announced. Would it make sense to give him a free pass and work to the next hitter?

The answer is on page 145.

12. THE NAME OF THE GAME

Easy one: What is, by far, the most important aspect of baseball, that is to say, if a team is strong in this department, it will usually win more than its share of contests? Is it:

1. A solid bench to spell your regulars
2. Pitching in general
3. A closer out of the bullpen
4. One or more sluggers in the middle of the lineup
5. Great gloves up the middle

The answer is on page 145.

13. STEAL SIGNS?

Is it legal within the rules of the game to steal signs from your opponents? If so, how would a manager use the intelligence his espionage team discovered?

The answer is on page 146.

14. WORLD SERIES CRUNCH TIME

Imagine it's the Fall Classic of 1962 and your hand is on the rudder of the Yankees (in reality, their manager was Ralph Houk). When the last of the ninth is finally reached in the Series finale, nerves are frayed and fingernails have long been chewed away. Your Yanks are nursing a 1–0 lead when the Giants rally and have Matty Alou on third and Willie Mays leading off second, representing the possible Series-winning run. To make matters worse, the monstrous Willie McCovey is in the batter's box with the solid-hitting Orlando Cepeda due next.

What do you do now? Walk McCovey, since his run means nothing, realizing, though, that the move would fill the bases and the peril of a run-scoring walk to Cepeda is palpable? Pitch to McCovey with righty Ralph Terry who is in the middle of twirling a four-hit shutout? Go to the bullpen to bring in a lefty to put out the McCovey fire?

The answer is on page 147.

15. MARATHON PITCHER

Here's a hypothetical situation. Randy Johnson is spinning a gem, with a two-hitter through seven innings. He's thrown an economical 98 pitches so far. If he manages to keep that pace up of around 14 pitches or so per inning, how long would you, playing the role of Johnson's manager Joe Torre, stick with him?

The answer is on page 147.

16. MARATHON, PART II

Let's change things up a bit. Say your starter gets bombed in the first inning so you replace him after a mere two outs have been recorded with a rubber-armed long relief man. Imagine that you come in with a guy like Tim Wakefield, normally a starter, but a guy who throws the knuckleball, which would allow him to work countless innings without tiring. Just how long would you use him?

The answer is on page 147.

17. DISCIPLINARY MATTERS

Part of a manager's job is that of a disciplinarian. During a Cleveland Indians game on September 23, 1999, Manny Ramirez, known for his stick but not for his glove, loafed while in pursuit of a foul fly ball that landed near the left field foul line. Tribe manager Mike Hargrove instantly knew that if Ramirez had hustled, he could have made the catch to retire a Tigers batter.

What action did Hargrove take?
1. He immediately yanked him from the contest
2. He waited for the inning to end, and then reprimanded Ramirez on the bench
3. He scolded him in private the next day
4. He fined him

The answer is on page 148.

18. GIVE HIM THE HOOK?

Nowadays, when a manager visits a pitcher on the mound during a tense moment, he has usually made up his mind to pull the pitcher. Put yourself in the place of Oakland A's manager Ken Macha during a 2004 contest. You've bolted out of the dugout, approached your starter, Mark Mulder, and now he's telling you he feels fine and wants to stay in the game. Do you go with your pitcher's testimony, or is it dangerous to set a precedent by allowing a player to talk you out of making a move?

The answer is on page 148.

19. SWING AWAY?

During an Indians game on June 17, 2001, Charlie Manuel was running the club and his pitcher, rookie C.C. Sabathia, was due up at the plate in an interleague game in Pittsburgh. With the bases loaded and one out, the Indians and Pirates were deadlocked at 0–0 in the fifth inning. As an American League pitcher, Sabathia seldom had the chance to swing a bat; he had only one big league at bat under his belt. In such a situation, would you pinch hit for him or allow him to hack away?

The answer is on page 148.

20. SWING AWAY, PART II

Having decided to stick with Sabathia, what did Manuel order when the count ran 3–1 to him while facing Pirates pitcher Todd Ritchie? Did he give him the take sign or allow him to use his own judgment on the next delivery?

The answer is on page 148.

21. C.C. ONE MORE TIME

On May 21, 2005, Sabathia, then hitting .273 over 22 lifetime at-bats, must have felt vindicated when he launched a game-winning, two-run homer to dead centerfield over the head of Ken Griffey, Jr. in a 5–3 win over the Cincinnati Reds. Three frames later, in the seventh, after he had thrown 102 pitches, he was due to lead off the inning. Manager Eric Wedge had a decision to make this time: Stick with him and let him bat, or replace him with a pinch hitter. Actually, he could have let Sabathia bat, seen the results, and then decided if he wanted to keep him on the mound. Say Sabathia hit a double. With Sabathia in scoring position, representing an important insurance run, Wedge could have then pinch run for the lumbering Sabathia. What would you do?

The answer is on page 148.

22. GREEN LIGHT?

It was the Cubs' Opening Day of 2000, and runners were on first and third with two outs and Sammy Sosa at the plate in the eighth inning. St. Louis led 7–1 when Eric Young began inching off first base, either to get a good two-out jump or possibly to swipe second.

Cardinals pitcher, right-hander Mark Thompson, pulled the old "fake a throw to third then whirl and fire the ball to first" move. And, even though it usually succeeds only in drawing derisive crowd reactions, this time it worked. Young was nailed. Why was this an utterly foolish move on Young's part and a big blow to the Cubs' chances?

The answer is on page 149.

23. PITCH COUNT MANIA

You are the Chicago Cubs manager Dusty Baker and the year is 2004. Your most pressing issue now may well be the critics who say you are using All-Star pitcher Carlos Zambrano too much. In today's game pitch counts are kept religiously and studied the same way.

Now, the 23-year-old Zambrano is a pretty big guy at 6'5" and 255 pounds, and he has said he could throw as many as 150 pitches in a game if called upon to do so. By early July he has gone over the 120-pitch mark in four of his last five starts. Do you, as his manager, start to back off now as the summer heats up?

The answer is on page 149.

24. MORE ROLE PLAY

Imagine you are Dusty Baker of 2004 once more, but this time you have to deal with the ego of your star slugger Sammy Sosa. Lamentably, Sosa is in the middle of a 13-game slump, hitting a meager .157 over that period. Not long ago you told the media that you were afraid of moving him lower in the batting order—he hadn't hit lower than the cleanup slot since July 8, 1994—because that move might lead to losing Sosa "psychologically or spiritually." Now, for the good of the club, you feel you must shove him down to the number five spot in the lineup. After all, of the 52 men who have hit cleanup with 100 or more at bats this season, Sosa's .220 batting average is the weakest. How do you break the news to him? In the days of "old school" baseball you might simply let him see his name on the lineup card and figure things out on his own; is that type of managing passé now?

The answer is on page 149.

25. SEPTEMBER CALLUPS

The year was 1973 and Oakland manager Dick Williams' roster was ripe. Due to the rule that allows teams to expand their rosters from the normal limit of 25 players come September 1, Williams had an abundance of second basemen, none known for their hitting skills, on the team. In the thick of a pennant race, Williams came up with a solution to his batting order's weak spot when his second baseman was due at the plate.

Did he: 1. Stick with the second sacker with the (relatively) hottest hand at the time; 2. Rotate a new second baseman into the lineup each night; or 3. Replace a second baseman by using a pinch hitter then plugging in a new man in the field every time one of his weak sticks had a turn at the plate?

The answer is on page 150.

26. FINAL CALL

In this scenario, you are manager Mike Hargrove of the Cleveland Indians. You have called upon your bench for a pinch hitter to replace star third baseman Travis Fryman in what would have been his last at bat in Tiger Stadium. Fryman, a former Tiger who hits right-handed, would love the opportunity to say farewell to his old ballpark and the Detriot fans who still appreciate what he had done in a Tigers uniform. The highly upset Fryman fumes on the bench, but Hargrove doesn't notice as he is simply making the move he feels would best benefit the Indians, using a left-handed pinch hitter to face a Detroit righty.

Now, the next day Hargrove learns from his coaches about Fryman's ire. What would you do in Hargrove's situation? Keep in mind, Fryman has the reputation as a consummate team player.

The answer is on page 150.

27. TO GO OR NOT TO GO

In May 2002, Cleveland's Omar Vizquel led off third base and Matt Lawton was on first with the Indians leading Baltimore, 4–1. With two men out and Travis Fryman at the plate facing Orioles pitcher Sean Douglass, who was working out of the stretch position, Vizquel took off for home on a straight steal. Is this play wise? Unconventional?

The answer is on page 150.

28. RUNNING WILD

Would you consider employing a triple steal—setting all three runners in motion with the bases loaded? After all, even if the lead runner is out at the plate, you'd still have two men in scoring position. Or is this play way too dicey?

The answer is on page 150.

29. HOW TO PITCH TO MCGWIRE

When Mark McGwire was setting home run records for frequency and for distance in the 1990s, Florida manager Jim Leyland was asked how to pitch to the muscular 6′ 5″, 250-pounder. He quipped, "I have no idea. Roll it up there and hope it doesn't bounce?"

What player has since forced managers to use the intentional walk strategy more than any man ever?

The answer is on page 151.

30. ALL-STARS

This manager had the task of constructing the lineup of his highly talented American League All-Star crew. Armed with a plethora of power hitters, he finally settled on using RBI machine Manny Ramirez as his cleanup hitter. A reporter asked a silly question about why Ramirez was handpicked to bat fourth when other Dominican-born players were available. The manager joked, "We don't base the lineup on nationalities. If we did, I would have had an Italian." Who is this manager?

The answer is on page 151.

31. SMOLTZ'S PICKER

The manager who guided the 2005 National League All-Star squad had this to say about one of his pitchers, John Smoltz: "I thought he was the best [closer] in our league [over the last few years]. Then he goes back to starting and is just remarkable." Smoltz made an appearance in the '05 mid-summer classic in Detroit, a fitting spot for the Michigan native whose grandfather was a member of the Tigers ground crew for close to 40 years. In addition, one of his uncles once had the job of placing numbers on the scoreboard at Tiger Stadium. Your job, however, is to identify the manager who left the 2005 game with a 3–1 record in All-Star play.

The answer is on page 151.

32. KEY TO SUCCESS

One of the keys to Rod Carew's success was his uncanny bat control, which he employed in capturing seven batting titles over his first 12 years in the majors. Using a light bat, he'd smoothly guide the ball to any hole in the defense. In addition, as one of his managers once observed, with only slight exaggeration, "He could bunt .300 if he tried." Who came up with that quote? Clue: He was a fiery, even volatile, manager and is most remembered for his tumultuous days with the Yankees both as a player and manager.

The answer is on page 151.

33. DOWN ON THE DEVIL RAYS

Since its inception in 1998, the Devil Rays franchise never went above .500 in the regular season until 2008, where they went all the way to the World Series. So abysmal were their first few years that, in 2001, it was fair to call Tampa Bay a downright terrible team. While in the midst of a 14-game meat grinder of a schedule, playing the formidable Yankees and Red Sox, the Devil Rays manager commented, "We're not intimidated by anyone . . . because we've been beaten by everybody." Who uttered those words of despair and self-mocking humor?

The answer is on page 151.

Chapter 7
ANSWERS

1. In theory, you absolutely never put a leadoff runner on in any inning. They say leadoff walks come around to score about 40 to 50 percent of the time, so to purposely give a pass to a batter is highly risky. Additionally, most skippers won't intentionally put the potential tying run on base, let alone the possible winning run. After all, what upside would there be to such moves?

However, that's exactly what McClendon instructed his team to do. McClendon's logic was simple: If the Pirates pitcher slipped and made one mistake, the torrid Bonds could easily homer and the Pirates would more than likely lose. However, working around Bonds allowed his staff to battle lesser hitters, taking their chances with them. Even though the Giants loaded the bases that frame, they failed to score and the Pirates went on to win, 8–6. The odd, brazen McClendon move worked.

2. A look at what happened on the Campanella play: With a payoff pitch due, the runner from first took off while the pitcher, not wanting to issue a walk that would move the potential game-winning runner into scoring position, knew he had to throw a strike. In such situations pitchers almost always serve up a fastball. Alston knew all this when he made his decision, and, sure enough, Campanella got his fastball, laced a long single to the outfield, and the Dodgers won the contest. If the pitcher had gotten cute and thrown a pitch off the plate, Campanella would simply have taken a free stroll to first.

Alston also knew that if Campanella had singled on the earlier 3–1 count, the runner off first would not have had the advantage of running on the pitch and would have wound up at third. The only danger of taking a 3–1 pitch was that Campy might whiff on the full count, but Alston was confident his hitter would see a good pitch to swing at.

3. Johnson did walk Bonds even though that loaded the bases and shoved two men into scoring position to make a tight spot in a close game even tighter. The next batter was Edgardo Alfonzo, who hit a line drive to Luis Gonzalez in left field, so the ploy worked. But wait! Gonzalez dropped the ball for a costly error. Furthermore, after center fielder Steve Finley, backing up the play, got to the ball, his throw back to shortstop Alex Cintron was low and skimmed off the grass. All three runners scored, busting the game wide open and the Giants waltzed to an 8–3 win.

   Bonds, by the way, is one of only six men to have been given an intentional walk with the bases loaded. The others were Abner Dalrymple in 1881, Nap Lajoie in 1901, Del Bissonette in 1928, Bill Nicholson in 1944, and, most recently, Josh Hamilton in 2008.

4. Often young, insecure managers will "cover themselves" by playing it safe and by utterly and completely going by the book. Nevertheless, established skippers such as Phil Garner have proven unafraid to take chances. Garner recalled how he'd go against the book with Jessie Orosco. "I'd bring him in to face a left-hander knowing that all the managers would bring in right-handers," said Garner, pointing out the opposing managers were, by making such a move, playing it 100 percent by the book.

   However, said Garner, "My book was the opposite with Jesse, and it worked with him. Jesse had much better numbers against right-handers. I can't tell you the number of times Jesse would get us a ground ball double play against right-handers."

5. Normally a team never tries to swipe third base with two outs since, with the runner at second already in scoring position and almost certain to cross home plate on a two-out hit, there is little to be gained in taking the chance of being gunned down at third. Still, explained Torre, "It's not necessarily a bad play to try to steal third here [Fenway Park] with two outs because it's

so tough to score with a single to left field from second because it's so shallow."

6. Muser recalls, "We needed a double play, and even though Gonzalez is leading the world in RBI, really, the only way out of the jam was a ground ball double play. So we walked Greer to set up our double play and we got our ground ball, but Gonzalez hit it in the seam between third and short, and we got beat.

   "Everybody says, 'Well, why do you walk Greer to pitch to the big RBI guy?' And I said, 'Because it's the only way out of this jam.' I had confidence that we could get a ground ball with a ground ball pitcher on the mound.

   "They [the media] thought I was stupid, but Johnny gave us an out by bunting. So we've got one out, now we're only two away from getting out of the jam. So, I will pitch into the meat of the order. I think once in awhile you have to do that; you can't pitch around people all the time."

7. Parrish played a hunch, and was delighted that "against Cincinnati, [our bad luck] went the other way. Vaughn was having trouble with the curve ball and even though he has hit Blair [well in the past], Blair should be a good match-up for him if he throws his breaking ball, so we brought Willie in and Willie struck him out."

8. Yes. The Tribe pitched to him, and the splendid first baseman made them pay. He drilled an 0–1 pitch, pulling it to right field for a three-run home run. For all intentions, the game was over.

   Manager Mike Hargrove explained his strategy to *The Plain Dealer*. He said the plan was to pitch around Palmeiro, but Nagy made a mistake, offering a pitch that was too tempting, way too fat.

   Hargrove said, "You pitch around guys all the time in the big leagues. It's an unintentional intentional walk. If we had fallen behind him, we would have walked him. There are times when you go against the book. I get hammered here a lot for going too much by the book. This time I went against the book, but it didn't work out." Such is the life of big league skippers.

9. Normally, that's the way to play this scenario out. Further, that's how Showalter handled it. However, when Anderson ripped a grand slam off the sidearming Brian Shouse, all was lost for Texas that day. Although Shouse had held Anderson hitless in their previous six encounters, Anderson actually was a .615 hitter versus lefty relievers on the year based on his eight hits, including two homers, in 13 at-bats.

10. The umpires were absolutely correct in their call and Berroa won't bat until the next time through the order.

   So, not only can't you protest the ruling, you have no one to blame but yourself for the faux pas. These kinds of mistakes shouldn't happen at the big league level, but, from time to time, they do.

   Bell confessed, "Checking the lineup card doesn't take much energy to do. The bottom line is, I didn't double-check the official lineup card with the card on the [dugout] wall. It's totally, totally my responsibility. It was inexcusable and irresponsible."

11. Walking him to place the potential winning run aboard seems foolhardy, but that's what Yankee skipper Bucky Harris did. The results were disastrous: The Dodgers countered with yet another pinch-hitter, Cookie Lavagetto, who promptly drilled a double to right, breaking up the no-hitter while clinching a 3–2 Brooklyn victory.

12. While every one of the multiple choices is important, the answer is 2—pitching plain and simple. Over the years experts have said that pitching is as high as 90 percent of the key to winning. In 2004 Larry Bowa, then manager of the Phillies, told *Philadelphia Inquirer* writer Todd Zolecki, "The name of the game is pitching

. . . If you want to look at box scores, all you have to do is look at the starting pitching on both teams. That's what it's all about. You get your starting pitcher to go seven innings, you get into your bullpen and you use your set-up guy and closer. That's how the game is supposed to be played."

In 1969 the upstart New York Mets, a pathetic franchise up to that point, startled the baseball world by transforming themselves into the "Amazin' Mets," World Series winners. Early in the year skeptics said the team's sticks were too weak for the team to go very far, pointing out that they had no big name hitters on their roster. Other than Cleon Jones, no starter topped the .280 plateau, and Tommie Agee, their top "slugger," hit only 26 homers with a feeble team-leading 76 RBI. What they did have, though, was outstanding pitching led by Tom Seaver, who led the league in wins with 25, and 17-game winner Jerry Koosman.

Most recently, the Atlanta Braves won an unprecedented 13 consecutive division titles. They did so with a pitching staff that placed either first or second in the entire majors for team ERA in an eye-popping 12 of those 13 magnificent seasons.

13. Stealing signs has been going on at the Major League level for decades upon decades. If a team isn't clever enough to disguise its signals, or if the enemy is sharp enough to decipher those signs, then a "spying" manager certainly will take advantage of the data.

One of the best in the business at stealing signs was Joe Nossek, with over 30 years' total experience as a player, minor league manager, and big league coach. While working under Milwaukee manager Del Crandall, Nossek frequently fed information that Crandall acted upon. For example, if Nossek's espionage had detected the steal sign, Crandall would call for a pitch out, giving his catcher a huge edge in trying to nail the runner.

Nossek added a secondary advantage to sign stealing. "I've been able to get a reputation for doing that, and it's served me well because even if you're not stealing anything, the psychological advantage may inhibit the other team at times."

Nossek also spoke about a cat-and-mouse game that took place when the Brewers met Texas, then under manager Billy Martin. "We had their signs, so I turned to Crandall and said, 'Billy's got the squeeze on.' So Del whistled to the catcher for a pitchout. Billy saw this and promptly took the squeeze off."

Since Nossek also noticed Martin make that countermove, the Brewers canceled the pitchout, and that prompted Martin to get "his third base coach's attention," to put the squeeze play on once more. Not to be outdone, Crandall called for the pitchout yet again.

Nossek said this went back and forth about three times. "Finally, Billy kept it on and we put the pitchout back on and got the runner at the plate. That was one of the few times we got the upper hand on Billy; he was good. He was smart so it was fun to go against him," said Nossek of the diamond's version of a multilayered chess game.

14. Houk had faith in Terry and allowed him to go right at McCovey. The slugger got a pitch to his liking and positively starched it, but the resulting fierce line drive headed directly towards and into the glove of second baseman Bobby Richardson. Game over. It was a "Whew!" moment for Houk and his Yankees to be sure, but they had boldly notched another world championship.

15. The answer is pretty much up to you with input from Johnson on how he feels. Typically nowadays, valuable starters don't toil for more than, say, 130 pitches, with pitch counts scrutinized under microscope-like attention.

16. Assuming you don't need him to make a start soon, Wakefield could easily give you as many innings as you might expect out of one of his starts. For the sake of argument, and to illustrate a point, let's just say he'd kill ten innings.

Now a real-life situation: On June 17, 1915, certainly in a different era, the Cubs' George "Zip" Zabel was summoned from the bullpen with two outs in the first and proceeded to pitch endless innings. Eventually, he won a 4–3 decision after 19 frames, the longest relief stint in Major League history. It is highly unlikely any man will ever again be called upon so long.

17. All the multiple choices make sense, but in this case Hargrove pulled him from the game. The next day, a seemingly contrite Ramirez pounded a grand slam and a three-run shot, good for a career-high eight ribbies in an 18–4 thrashing of Toronto.

18. Somewhat surprisingly, Macha said that when he spoke with Mulder he would get the truth out of him (unlike many pitchers who refuse to admit they're floundering).

   "I trust Mark 1,000 percent," said Macha.

19. Manuel let him take his cuts and later explained with a grin, "C.C. is a good hitter. Go ask him. He'll tell you he's a good hitter." Sabathia commented that he was pretty good in high school with a bat in his hands. "If you don't hit .400 in high school, you're not doing much. But that was two years ago. Now I'm facing a 94 mph fastball."

20. Although he took some heat for his call, Manuel let him hit away. Unfortunately for the Indians, Sabathia hit the ball sharply on the ground to third base for the start of an around-the-horn double play to end the inning and to kill the only real scoring opportunity on the night; the Pirates prevailed, 1–0.

   Sabathia commented that he wasn't given a take sign, then added, "I mean, I don't know the signs, but I'm sure if they wanted me not to swing, Joel Skinner [third base coach] would have yelled to me."

21. Wedge, frustrated with this team's lethargic offense around that time of the season, let his starting pitcher bat. After he grounded

out, Wedge gave him the night off and went to the bullpen. "I didn't want to use another player," explained Wedge of his unusual move, "and C.C. had certainly hit the guy well in his previous at bat. There was no harm in letting him have another chance."

22. What's the advantage of Eric Young stealing? Down by six runs, a stolen base would be meaningless, hardly worth the chance of getting caught stealing or, worse, picked off. If he wasn't thinking of stealing, then straying too far off base was absolutely ludicrous. Additionally, by making the third out of the inning, he took the bat out of Sosa's hands in a situation where a home run could have drawn the Cubs closer to the Cards.

23. Baker observed that the critics were "not questioning" the pitch count on Carlos, "they're questioning the pitch count on me. People go way overboard with this pitch count. What happened before the pitch count? It just gives something else for people to write about or talk about. And it gives them something else to second-guess and ridicule the manager about." Still, pitchers' arms are highly valuable commodities and, as such, must be protected.

24. Nowadays not even hard-line managers would treat a star in "old school" fashion. Baker called Sosa into his office and suggested the move. Baker announced that Sosa indicated that "it would be better for the team and the way he's going to drop him down in the order . . . He said he wanted to do what was best for the team to help us get to the playoffs and to the World Series." Players of Sosa's standing do get special treatment, and do get coddled. The short-term results of the switch were positive with Sosa homering in two of his next three games. Long range, it didn't matter as the Cubs did not make post season play and Sosa and the Cubs became alienated—he moved on to become a member of the 2005 Baltimore Orioles.

By the way, in the first game after the 2005 All-Star game Sosa, hitting just .225, was moved out of his customary five hole in the lineup. Manager Lee Mazzilli actually inserted Sosa into the second slot in his order, of all places. Sosa went 0–for–4 with a sac fly while striking out three times.

25. 3. In a clever and unique move, for the season's final three weeks, Williams used four second basemen every game. By the way, his A's wound up winning the pennant.

26. You should (and Hargrove did) salvage Fryman's sore ego. Hargrove, also a class act, called Fryman in, explained what his thought process had been, and apologized to his third baseman. Fryman accepted the mea culpa and it was reported that the rest of the Indians, who were sympathetic to their buddy Fryman, appreciated Hargrove's actions.

27. Don't blame the manager in this instance. First of all, Vizquel went on his own so Fryman might have been swinging away, perhaps even injuring Vizquel. Fryman later commented, "I saw Omar out of the corner of my eye . . . It did catch me off guard, though." He added, "Normally you only try it when the pitcher is using the windup. I guess it's a good play if you make it."

Cleveland manager Charlie Manuel commented, "I had no problem with it. Why not do it there? Give the other team something to think about. When I managed in the minor leagues, we would always run all of our plays the first time through the league just to show the other teams everything we had so they had something to think about the rest of the season." Therefore, it was probably not a very smart baseball move, but a bold one to be sure.

28. While rare, pulling off a triple steal certainly has been done. In one case, Minnesota's Rod Carew was on third, Tony Oliva led off second, and Harmon Killebrew was nestled in at first. All three took off against Seattle pitcher Bucky Brandon, and all three made it. By the way, Carew's steal was one of a record-tying seven times he pilfered home (out of eight attempts) in 1969. The Twins under manager Billy Martin pulled off another triple steal with Carew as the lead runner later that year.

That season Martin loved his base runners to scoot freely. He had them burgle five bases in a matter of a few pitches on May 18, 1969. The onslaught began when Cesar Tovar stole third. Then, after Carew drew a walk, Tovar pulled off a double steal with him. Shortly after that, Carew stole third and home.

29. Barry Bonds. In 2004, he drew an ungodly record-setting 232 bases on balls. By way of comparison, the most Ruth ever earned was 170, a stunning total before the Bonds era. Furthermore, 120 of Bonds' walks were intentional, yet another new record which far eclipsed marks set by previous record holders (the American League record is a mere 33). Entering the 2007 season, Bonds had amassed 2,558 career walks (number one all-time), leaving former record holders such as Rickey Henderson and Babe Ruth far behind.

30. Boston Red Sox skipper Terry Francona, obviously of Italian decent, made that observation.

31. The NL manager was Tony La Russa.

32. Billy Martin.

33. Hal McRae.

Chapter 8
The Front Office

PULLING THE STRINGS

It's time to kick off your sneakers and don a three-piece suit for your job as general manager. Can you earn your pay as a front office executive?

1. PITCHER WITH HEAT VS. HOT CORNER ALL-STAR

The New York Mets had trouble finding a quality third baseman basically from their first day of existence. After the 1971 season, they decided to make a trade to fill that need. They acquired veteran Jim Fregosi, a six-time All Star, from the California Angels in return for Leroy Stanton, Don Rose, Francisco Estrada, and a young flame-throwing pitcher. This wound up being one of the most lopsided trades ever, as the pitcher in question went on to become a Hall of Famer. Imagine what he could have accomplished had he stayed there and worked alongside Tom Seaver and Jerry Koosman. Name the pitcher.

The answer is on page 157.

2. SPEED VS. VETERAN HURLERS

In what is generally regarded as one of the worst front office moves ever, the Chicago Cubs traded for two veteran St. Louis pitchers, Ernie Broglio and Bobby Shantz, but in return surrendered a future Hall of Fame speed demon. Who was the youngster they gave up on way too early?

The answer is on page 157.

3. PLUGGING A HOLE

In 2004, the Houston Astros had the opportunity to obtain Carlos Beltran from the Kansas City Royals. Now, if you were the Astros general manager, knowing that Beltran was going to be a free agent at the end of the season, would you "rent a player" to help you down the stretch run, perhaps propelling you into the postseason?

The answer is on page 157.

4. SWAP HIM?

Just days before the 1982 season began, the Texas Rangers sent a hard-hitting outfielder to the Montreal Expos for Larry Parrish and Dave Hostetler. Parrish gave the Rangers six productive seasons, including two with 100 or more RBI. Hostetler spent three years with Texas, with '82 being his best showing (only .232, but with 67 RBI). Even though the Expos new outfielder lasted only two seasons with them, in 1982 he led the National League in hits, doubles, runs driven in, and batting average. Whether this deal favored the Expos or the Rangers is debatable; your call is to identify the man who went on to win the batting crown in his debut season with the Expos. Was it:
1. Al Oliver
2. Andre Dawson
3. Tim Raines
4. Warren Cromartie

The answer is on page 158.

5. UNIQUE TRADE

Only once in the annals of the game has a reigning batting crown winner been traded for the winner of the home run crown. Name the principals in this deal.

The answer is on page 158.

6. A-ROD WORTH IT?

On January 26, 2001, the Texas Rangers signed Alex Rodriquez as a free agent, almost exactly three months after he was granted

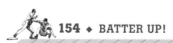

free agency status, cutting his ties with the Mariners. He stayed deep in the heart of the Lone Star state until February 16, 2004, when he was peddled to the Yankees in exchange for Alfonso Soriano and cash. During his three-season Texas stay, he earned a staggering $66 million. Was he worth all that loot?

The answer is on page 158.

7. ANOTHER MORTGAGING-THE-FUTURE SCENARIO

Down the stretch run of the 1987 pennant race, the Detroit Tigers felt that if they could pick up a dependable veteran pitcher, they could win their division. After trade talks between Atlanta and Detroit went on for some time, a deal was consummated. The Tigers got veteran Doyle Alexander for a young John Smoltz. Would you have made this swap?

The answer is on page 159.

8. TURNABOUT

The 2003 Detroit Tigers were positively hapless, but they were able to transform themselves into a respectable team in just one year by making a few moves. They picked up a bullpen closer in Ugueth Urbina, but their acquisitions of an established star behind the plate and a fine shortstop were key pickups. Name either of these men.

The answer is on page 159.

9. BACK-TO-BACK MVP AWARDS

In 1972, the Cincinnati Reds were ripped by their fans for shipping Lee May, Tommy Helms, and Jimmy Stewart to Houston. The Reds added four players to their roster who would go on to form a nucleus for their success in the "Big Red Machine" era, proving once more that trades cannot be evaluated on the spot. In addition to Ed Armrister, Jack Billingham, and Cesar Geronimo, what future Hall of Fame infielder and winner of consecutive MVP trophies did the Reds gain in this huge trade?

The answer is on page 160.

10. ANOTHER BIG FAUX PAS

The Philadelphia Phillies gave up on this young right-hander when they made a deal with the Cubs in 1966. Chicago shrewdly surrendered aging pitchers Bob Buhl and Larry Jackson, and both were finished within three years. In the meantime, their new acquisition won 147 games as a Cub, won the 1971 Cy Young Award, and mowed down 1,808 batters while with the Cubbies. Name this pitcher.

The answer is on page 160.

Chapter 8
ANSWERS

1. It was a young Nolan Ryan. Over his time spent with the Mets, he won just 29 games; over his next three seasons with the Angels, he averaged just over 20 victories a year with untouchable strikeout totals: 329, the all-time record high of 383, and 367. He was off and running, on his way to 324 wins and a staggering 5,714 whiffs. In the meantime, Fregosi lasted only one full season (.232 and just 32 RBI) with the Mets before they dumped him in 1973 after only 45 games.

2. The Cubs served Lou Brock up on a platter to the Cardinals, where he stayed as an institution from the day of the trade in 1964 through the end of his career in 1979. Over that span he registered over 3,000 hits, burgled 938 bases—the all-time best until Rickey Henderson came along—and helped guide the Cards to three World Series appearances. Broglio and Shantz were pretty good pitchers, but by the time of the transaction they were over the hill. Broglio won seven games for the Cubs in two and a half seasons and Shantz lasted only 20 games (0–1) for Chicago.

3. When a team makes a move that may help them short term, but perhaps hurts them long range, they are said to have "mortgaged their future." In some cases, when trying to determine if a move was worth it or not, one should wait many years before looking back to make a judgment.

   In the Astros' case, you decide, but here are the facts to date: 1) They made the playoffs with Beltran contributing big time. Overall, he drove in 104 runs and fell just short of becoming the fourth member of the 40 home run/40 stolen base club. In the Astros uniform, he hit 23 homers and scored 70 runs in a mere 90 games. 2) For the first time since their inception in 1962, the

Astros made it to the second round of the postseason and did so largely thanks to Beltran's record four homers in the Division Series versus Atlanta. 3) Ultimately, Houston lost to St. Louis, but only after Beltran tied playoff records with his totals of eight homers and 14 RBI to go with his .435 average. 4) Before the start of 2005, the Astros lost Beltran through free agency to the New York Mets, who agreed to pay him over $11.5 million for the 2005 season.

4. 1. Al Oliver. Incidentally, twice in baseball history a team has swapped a player during a season and that man went on to win that season's batting title. It happened in 1932 when the Tigers sent Dale Alexander (after he had only 16 at bats with them) to the Red Sox and in 1947 when Harry "The Hat" Walker was dealt from the Cardinals (after just 25 at bats there) to the Phillies.

5. Prior to the 1960 season, Rocky Colavito was sent packing by general manager Frank "Trader" Lane to Detroit for Harvey Kuenn. Kuenn was coming off a marvelous .353 season, but Cleveland fans didn't care about that—they were livid. The beloved Colavito had just drilled 42 homers and chased home 111 runs. Colavito, too, was outraged. He commented, "The trade came as a great shock. It was a trade that never should have happened. I got dumped."

What made matters worse was that Colavito went on to average more that 32 homers a year for the next seven seasons. By contrast, Kuenn lasted only one year with the Indians.

6. It's your call, but, once more, here are some basic facts: Over that span the Rangers were in fourth place each year, failing each season to break .500. Over the eight previous seasons before A-Rod's arrival they finished first four times, second once, third two times, and fourth once, in 2000. The year he departed the Rangers went from fourth to third place in the standings. Clearly, he was no savior.

Rodriguez was, however, as always, a superstar. His stats glistened: He played 162 games each year despite laboring under the draining, blistering, and unforgiving Texas sun. He crushed 52, 57, and 47 home runs and delivered well over 100 RBI yearly with a high of 142 in 2002. He hit over .300 with a slugging percentage over .600 during his tenure as a Ranger. What more could he have done?

Was it his fault the club didn't have enough support to win more frequently? Again, in this case, it's your call.

7. One can look at this deal two ways: Any chance you have to make it to the playoffs with a legitimate chance to win it all, you must seize the day. From the day of the deal, August 12, through the end of the season, Alexander, who had been 5–10 for the Braves, sizzled. His unblemished 9–0 slate with a spectacular ERA of 1.53 helped ignite the Tigers, who won the East Division but fell short of a World Series appearance when the Twins knocked them off in the ALCS.

The trade has to be considered a flop if one reviews what Smoltz went on to achieve. Twenty-one seasons after the swap, Smoltz had 210 wins and 154 saves for Atlanta. Both of those figures are more than any Tigers pitcher accumulated over that time frame. As a matter of fact, the most victories the most successful Tigers hurler accumulated over that span was 61 by Frank Tanana, some 149 fewer than Smoltz! He is the only man ever to be effective enough as a starter to notch 15 shutouts while also being so sharp as a reliever that he compiled 150-plus saves. Not only that, the 1996 Cy Young Award winner has been a mainstay of the Braves who, through 2005, made it to the playoffs every year since 1991. He is, in fact, the only player to have been a part of each and every one of those title teams. Finally, from May 29, 2002 until May 26, 2003, the Braves never lost a game in which Smoltz pitched. That covered a period of 72 straight wins, a big league record. In short, Alexander was a big help for one year, but Smoltz has been "money" for an eon.

8. The Tigers front office aggressively went after and signed catcher Ivan Rodriguez as a free agent to a hefty contract (just over $6.5 million in 2004) and picked up new shortstop Carlos Guillen. Shortly after the All-Star break, on July 18, 2004, the Tigers had surpassed their victory total from the entire 2003 season and still had two and a half months left to play. Sure, they were only playing near the .500 level, but it was a considerable improvement over their showing in 2003 when they set a new American League record for losses, going 43–119. They also established a record for the fewest games needed to go beyond their win total from the previous year, needing just 91 games, some 15 fewer than the previous record holders. In all, their win total ascended by nearly 30, up to 72 victories in 2004.

9. The future Hall of Fame infielder and two-time MVP trophy winner was second baseman Joe Morgan.

10. The Cub who won the 1971 Cy Young Award was Fergie Jenkins.

Chapter 9
The Rules

TOUGH CALLS

See if you can come up with answers and/or rulings on some very strange plays.

1. PITCHER DECEPTION

Pedro Martinez of the New York Mets is on the hill with enemy runners off first and third with, say, two outs. Martinez would like to get out of the inning the easy way, by picking off a runner rather than face the risk of offering up a juicy pitch to the batter. Is he permitted to fake a throw to third, swivel, and then fire the ball to first, perhaps catching a napping runner straying off the bag too far?

The answer is on page 182.

2. ODD INNING?

Is it possible for a team to lay down three sacrifice bunts in an inning? If so, has it ever happened in the Major Leagues?

The answer is on page 182.

3. ODD INNING? PART II

Is it conceivable for a team to hit three sacrifice flies in an inning?

The answer is on page 182.

4. GO FOR TWO

When Larry Rothschild was the Tampa Bay manager, he thought back to a trick play from his days in uniform with Cincinnati. His Reds took on the Giants under manager Roger Craig who "had a bunt play where, with first and second occupied, the third base man charged and the shortstop went to [cover] second base." Judging from the defensive setup mentioned, can you ascertain what the Giants were trying to pull off?

The answer is on page 183.

5. BILLY MARTIN TRICK PLAY

Longtime Braves coach Pat Corrales said, "Billy Martin had that bunt play when he had a left-handed hitter up. Rickey Henderson would take off stealing and the guy would bunt the ball to third base and Henderson wouldn't even think about stopping at second. He'd continue to third base." What name is given to such a play?

The answer is on page 183.

6. SNEAK IN AND OUT

One tricky play that can work well at the amateur level goes like this: The shortstop works his way behind a runner off second base then breaks for the bag; the pitcher intentionally ignores the shortstop's pleas for a throw. Acting disgusted as if a sneak-in play had been blown, the fielder loops in front of the runner, making his way back to his shortstop position.

At that moment, hoping the runner is lulled into a sense of safety, the second basemen darts in behind the runner and this time a pickoff throw comes his way. Would such a play work in the big leagues?

The answer is on page 183.

7. MINOR LEAGUE SLEIGHT OF HAND

Roberto Alomar has run his share of trick plays, but there was one he saw in the minors that floored him. "It was around 1986," he began, "with somebody at first base and the pitcher threw the ball over there [on a pickoff move]. Then a guy who was on the bench rolled a ball out toward the outfield. The guy who was diving back to first base looked up; he saw the ball rolling away. The first baseman started going after that ball. When he did that, the runner started going to second [thinking the pickoff throw had been errantly fired into shallow right field]."

Once the runner began his dash, he was picked off easily, with the first baseman producing the "real" ball and making an easy lob for the out. Is this play legal?

The answer is on page 184.

8. AN OLDIE

Infielder Kevin Stocker recalled a play he thought was very creative from his days in the minor leagues. "When you had a guy on first base and a right-handed hitter was up, our catcher would catch the ball [on each pitch] and throw it back to the pitcher every time the same way [over and over and over]. Then, without even looking, he could come up and throw to first, but still be looking at the pitcher [as he had done on every throw earlier].

"The guy on first base oftentimes would just think, 'Oh, he's throwing it back to the pitcher.' He'd lower his head and kind of walk to the base at the same time the ball got there and we'd tag him out." Other than the deception involved, what does it take on the catcher's part to make the play succeed?

The answer is on page 184.

9. SQUEEZE

Which league tends to use the squeeze play more, the National or the American, and why?

The answer is on page 184.

10. KINGS OF TRICK PLAYS

Bobby Cox, through 2005 a four-time winner of the Manager of the Year Award, has cited two managers as creators of great trick plays. Do you know who they are?

1. Danny Murtaugh
2. Billy Martin
3. Gene Mauch
4. Tony La Russa
5. Sparky Anderson

The answer is on page 185.

11. EVERY LITTLE EDGE

Just for fun, let's turn the clock back to 2004, when the Yankee-Bosox rivalry was reaching its boiling point yet. Boston's Johnny Damon is on third base and Yankees pitcher Mike Mussina is working out of the windup, paying little attention to Damon. Mark Bellhorn is the batter, and, realizing the steal of home has been called for, he decides to slightly change his position in the batter's box. Where would he move that would give an oh-so-slight edge to Damon in his attempt to swipe home?

The answer is on page 186.

12. HANK SET HIM UP

Harry "The Hat" Walker managed Roberto Clemente and had many opportunities to see Hank Aaron in action, too. Walker said that Aaron was the better of the two players and that while Clemente was regarded as the better fielder, Aaron was under-appreciated in that realm.

Walker then recalled that when Aaron was on the base paths he occasionally "baited Clemente." What deception did Aaron carry out on Clemente?

The answer is on page 186.

13. YOU'RE THE OFFICIAL SCORER ONCE MORE

Texas Rangers reliever Scott Bailes entered the game against the Mariners who had two men out in the top of the ninth. He made two deliveries to Seattle's Rob Ducey, then picked Russ Davis off first base. The Rangers rallied in the bottom of the ninth inning to win it. Does Bailes get a win, a save, or neither?

The answer is on page 186.

14. THE FALLEN

With runners on second and third and one out, the batter hits a foul pop near the third-base dugout. The third baseman makes a spectacular catch and then falls into the fenced-off area for photographers. The runner from third base tags up and scores. The runner from second tags up and tries to advance, but the third baseman recovers and manages to get the ball to a teammate, who tags the runner out at third.

Is this a valid double play? Does the run count?

The answer is on page 187.

15. ROLL ON

A batter hits a high fly ball that falls, untouched, on the slope of the pitcher's mound and then rolls all the way across the third-base foul line, where it is picked up by the shortstop.

Is the ball fair or foul?

The answer is on page 188.

16. BALL IN POCKET

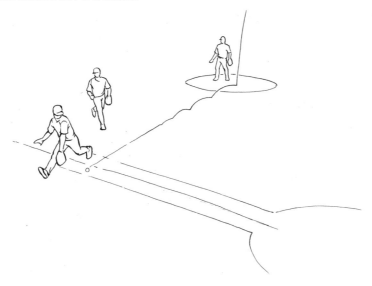

The runner from third base breaks for home plate when a wild pitch gets away from the catcher. The ball lands in the umpire's pocket, and for a few seconds no one can find it—not even the umpire!

Does the ball remain in play? If not, are the base runners allowed to advance?

The answer is on page 188.

17. NOT PLAYING THE BAG WELL

A runner leads off first base when the pitcher, with his pivot foot still in contact with the rubber, attempts a pick-off by throwing to the first baseman. But the ball glances off the first baseman's mitt and rolls into the dugout.

How many bases is the runner awarded?

The answer is on page 189.

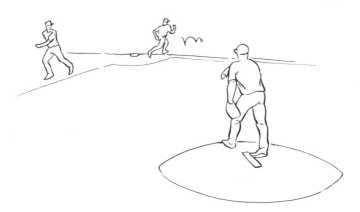

18. A TIP FROM ME

There is a man on first base with no outs. The count on the batter is 3–2. On the next pitch, the runner is moving, the batter swings, and the umpire calls a foul tip.

Is the batter out? Does the runner have to go back to first base?

The answer is on page 189.

19. AN "IDIOT" ON THE BASEPATHS

The runner on first base makes a dash for second with a 3–1 count on the batter. The pitch comes in as ball four. Meanwhile, the catcher makes the throw to second base just in case the pitch was called a strike. The runner slides into second ahead of the throw, but then steps off momentarily toward center field as the shortstop continues to hold the tag on him.

Is the runner out or does he remain at second base because of the walk?

The answer is on page 190.

20. JUST PASSING THROUGH

With runners on first and second and no one out, the batter hits the ball over the fence in left field. The runner from second base takes a few steps and watches the ball, thinking that it might be caught. In the meantime, the runner from first base puts his head down and runs past his teammate.

Is either runner called out on this play? Does it still count as a home run?

The answer is on page 190.

21. SNEAKING AROUND

With two outs and runners on first and second, the batter hits a ground ball to the right side of the infield. The second baseman fields the ball and throws to the pitcher, who is running to cover first base while the first baseman is out of position. The pitcher catches the throw and beats the batter to first, but the umpire rules the runner safe because the pitcher failed to step on the bag. The pitcher, however, believes that his foot caught the edge of the base, and he argues with the first-base umpire. In the meantime, the other runners continue around the base-paths and cross home plate.

During an argument with the umpire, can runners advance?

The answer is on page 191.

22. COUNTING TO THREE

The bases are loaded with one out when the batter hits a routine fly ball. The left fielder catches it and, thinking there are now three outs, hands the ball to a young fan. When he sees the runners tagging up, he grabs the ball back from the startled spectator and throws to home plate, but by then two runs have scored.

Could all three runners have scored if the fan kept the ball for himself?

The answer is on page 191.

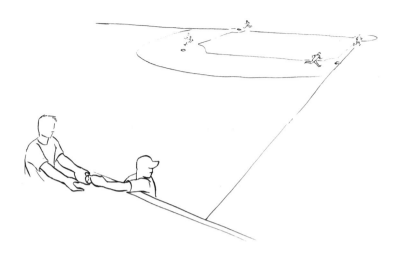

23. DESIGNATED MADNESS

During the late innings of an American League contest, the home team's manager sends the designated hitter in to play in the outfield. To make room for him, an outfielder leaves the game.

Once the designated hitter comes in to play defense, can another player become the designated hitter or does the pitcher have to bat? Whatever you think the answer is, will the new designated hitter or pitcher then bat in place of the original designated hitter or in place of the player who has left the game?

The answer is on page 192.

THE APPEAL OF THE GAME

A good understanding of the appeal play can make the difference between losing or winning a game. Let's see how familiar you are with the rules governing this simple yet often-misunderstood play.

DEFINITION: APPEAL PLAY

An appeal play is when the defense claims that the offense violated the rules. Some appeal plays can be made verbally, while others require special actions like stepping on a base while in possession of the ball. If the defense does not appeal or appeals incorrectly, then play proceeds as if no violation took place.

24. HOWE TO APPEAL

With runners on first and third and one out, the batter hits a deep fly ball to center field. Just before the ball is caught, the runner on third takes off for home, scoring easily. The runner on first stays where he is. Seeing that the runner from third left early, the defense tries to organize an appeal play.

The pitcher takes the ball while standing on the rubber. He steps off, walks a few steps to third, and throws the ball to the third baseman. But the throw is wild and bounces into the stands. The plate umpire gives the pitcher a new ball, and he tries to appeal again, this time successfully making the throw to third.

On the overthrow, is the runner from first base awarded any additional bases, even though he was not trying to advance on the play? Is this a proper appeal, and should the runner from third be called out, nullifying the run?

The answer is on page 193.

25. THE GHOST RUN

Runners are on first and third with one out. The batter attempts to bunt but pops up to the pitcher. Both runners are trying to advance and are well off their bases when the ball is caught. The pitcher then throws to the first baseman to record the third out. Pleased that the double play ends the half-inning, the defense

leaves the field. But in the meantime, the runner from third, who never retouched his base after the out, had crossed home plate before the out at first.

Does the run count?

The answer is on page 196.

DEFINITION: FORCE OUT

A force out can occur when a runner loses his right to his base because the batter becomes a runner (usually after hitting the ball). Runners are forced when there is no open base between them and the batter. Force outs can be recorded by tagging the runner or tagging the base to which he is advancing.

26. TOUCHING THEM ALL

A runner leads off first base with one out when the batter hits a line drive. The third baseman catches the ball and then tries for a double play by throwing to first, where the runner has not tagged up and is off the base. But the throw is wild and goes out of play. The umpires call time and award the runner two bases on the overthrow.

When the ball is dead on an overthrow, can the runner still return to his base to tag up? Does he need to tag up or does

the overthrow nullify the defense's chance to appeal? What are the two bases awarded to him—first and second, or second and third?

The answer is on page 198.

ORDER OF THE DAY

In cases of batting out of order, at least one of the two managers is guilty of the kind of mistake that can cost his team the game. It is tough to know what is more surprising—that this happens as often as it does or that so few managers have figured out how to use the rule to their advantage. Either way, it has led to some funny situations. Here are two.

27. FROM CIRCLE TO BOX

Runners are on second and third with one out when the batter hits a sacrifice fly to score the man from third base. The problem is that this batter was not due up yet. According to the lineup, he should have been in the on-deck circle rather than the batter's box. Following this, the batter whose turn had just been skipped comes in to hit.

Is the play allowed to stand, despite the batting out of order?

The answer is on page 200.

28. INVISIBLE DOUBLE SWITCH

The home team's manager replaces his shortstop and pitcher in the top of the seventh, but he does not indicate to the umpire where these players will bat in the batting order. The umpire assumes that they will each bat in the place of the person whose defensive position they are replacing. In the bottom of the seventh, with the pitcher due up, the shortstop comes in and hits a double. The visiting manager appeals for batting out of order.

Does the double still count? Is either the shortstop or the pitcher called out?

The answer is on page 201.

◆ ◆ ◆

FANS AND THE FIELD

Let's explore the rules that define what is acceptable conduct by both players and their fans.

29. FANS 3, LAW AND ORDER 0

Between games of a doubleheader, the home team decides to provide some on-field entertainment, which quickly leads to a riot that makes the field unplayable.

Is the second game postponed or is a forfeit awarded to the visitors?

The answer is on page 203.

30. A SECOND LOOK

After hitting a difficult groundball to the shortstop, the batter thinks he made it safely to first base. But the umpire calls him out. The batter is clearly upset and asks the umpire to check the instant replay.

After the batter asks to check the television replay, what should the umpire do?

1. Agree to the request in order to make sure he got the call right
2. Explain that there is no use of instant replay in baseball
3. Eject the batter from the game

The answer is on page 205.

31. REVENGE

It is a close game between two archrivals. In the fifth inning, the visiting pitcher hits a batter. One inning later, the home team's pitcher throws a pitch that hits a visiting batter.

What is the automatic penalty when the second batter is hit?

The answer is on page 205.

32. TRIPPING

In just 1⅓ innings, a starting pitcher issues five walks, hits a batter, and gives up four hits and four runs. Three of the runs score on bases-loaded walks. This performance inspires the pitching coach to make a trip to the mound. While the coach is out there, he makes a loud comment about the plate umpire's strike zone and is ejected from the game. The team's manager then emerges to try to break up the ensuing argument. While on the field, the manager also speaks to the pitcher.

The umpires decide that manager's brief discussion with the pitcher constitutes a second trip to the mound during the same at-bat. Does the pitcher have to leave the game immediately?

The answer is on page 206.

33. HE'S GOT A POINT

The batter hits a hard ground ball that bounces very close to the third base bag and goes to the outfield corner, rolling into foul territory. The third base umpire points toward fair territory, signaling a fair ball. The batter makes it into second base for a double. The third baseman thinks the ball was foul and points to the place just outside the third base bag where he thinks the ball struck the ground.

Has the third baseman committed an offense?

The answer is on page 207.

Chapter 9
ANSWERS

1. While pitchers can't fake a throw to an empty base or, for that matter, fake a throw to first (those moves would be called balks), what is described here is perfectly legal but very, very rarely works.

   However, veteran pitcher Wilson Alvarez said he's not only seen it succeed, but he played with an expert at it when he was with the Chicago White Sox. "Oh, yeah," he smiled, "I saw that play many times with Jack McDowell. He used to pick off like four or five guys a year like that. I think he was the best in the league at that." He went so far as to say that this play works more often than one might expect at the Major League level.

2. Yes, three sac bunts in an inning can happen and has occurred—14 times in all through June of 2005. The most recent took place on June 26th of 2005 when the Texas Rangers met their interstate rivals, the Houston Astros, in interleague play. Normally, every sacrifice bunt results in an out, so three in an inning seems impossible—the third out on a bunt would negate the scoring of that play as a sacrifice. However, in this instance, it was possible because Texas first baseman Mark Teixeira made a throwing error on one of the bunt plays, so naturally no out occurred there and the seventh inning wound up featuring three sac bunts!

3. Three sacrifice flies have been hit by one team in an inning. Here's the most recent time three sac flies were tagged in the majors—the first time ever in National League play.

   Marlon Anderson of the Mets singled off the glove of Yankees first baseman Tino Martinez to start a wild second inning on June 24, 2005. Mike Mussina then issued a walk to David Wright and gave up a Doug Mientkiewicz bunt single down the third base line to load the bags. At that point, Ramon Castro's sac fly to

Gary Sheffield in right tied the game 1–1 and allowed Wright to scamper to third. Jose Reyes followed with another sacrifice fly, which was also ruled an error when Bernie Williams misplayed the ball, taking his eyes off the ball then dropping it. So the run scored on the sacrifice, but the batter lived at first on the big E, and there was still only one out.

The record-setting fly came after Mussina's error on a pickoff attempt permitted Reyes and Mientkiewicz to advance to second and third. Mike Cameron completed the zany inning when he lofted a fly to Sheffield, allowing Mientkiewicz to score off a dazed Mussina.

4. Rothschild said if the team bunted the ball to third, and most teams tried to do just that, a hard-charging third baseman would seize the ball "and they'd throw to second base to try to [start] the double play to get out of an inning. It was an unusual play and it worked a couple of times." Getting the lead man at second wasn't too tough, but they'd succeed in turning a twin killing if they employed the play under ideal circumstances. For example, said Rothschild, "We had a slow runner, Joe Oliver, [at the plate] which you have to have to try to get a double play there. It was the first time we'd seen the play and it happened twice in a series and it worked both times."

5. Corrales said it was basically a bunt and run and "instead of one base [on the bunt], they'd get two bases." Corrales, by the way, said that the Braves don't go for tricks as a rule, realizing they can often backfire on a team. Half-jokingly he said the best "trick is not to let the guy get to first base."

6. Wilson Alvarez offered his mixed opinion: "At this level, whatever it takes. It might work, but we [really] don't use it." In other words, he seems to think it never hurts to try some sleight of hand, but felt this particular one seems better suited for much lower levels of play.

Nevertheless, Baltimore's Cy Young Award winner Mike Flanagan said his team actually used to run similar plays. "At second base we used a combination pickoff [much like the play described above] with the second baseman and shortstop. The second baseman would go [to the bag to take the first pickoff throw]. Then, as soon as that play ended, the second baseman would start leaving; then the shortstop would come in behind— that was a little bit different." The play hinged on the fact that as soon as the runner began to once more "take his lead, then our shortstop would come in" and trap the complacent runner on the second throw.

The Orioles, under legendary skipper Earl Weaver, attempted, said Flanagan, "a lot of different pickoff plays. We'd also put the first baseman behind the runner [at first] and have a timing play [with the fielder sneaking in at first to take the pitcher's pickoff throw]."

7. No, but believe it or not, Alomar recalls the defense "got away with it."

8. According to Stocker, "It takes a good arm from the catcher to be able to come up and just kind of flick it toward first [in the manner of his other throws]. The idea is not to come up and fire it. The idea is to keep the same motion and just kind of flick it. The rhythm has got to be the same. Of course, the first baseman's gotta be ready, too. It's not really a set play, it takes everyone being alert." Everyone, that is, except the runner who "you can kinda get him sleeping."

9. Neither league uses this trick play as much as they used to in, say, the dead ball era, but Wilson Alvarez commented, "They don't use it a lot in the American League. Once, maybe twice a year; they always play for the big innings." One reason the "Junior Circuit" doesn't tend to play for a run here and a run there is that they employ a designated hitter. So, with one additional strong stick in their lineup, they shy away from giving away outs, which takes place on most squeeze plays. Instead, they send their heavy artillery to the plate and take their chances on scoring runs in bulk.

One manager disagreed somewhat. Larry Rothschild said he ran the play with the Devil Rays. "It depends on your team and if you have the right elements in place. Good plays are made by players being able to perform different things. If the squeeze is going to put you ahead going into the ninth inning, you take your chance with it. If that means you're going to get the lead by squeezing, then you take the chance and do it. Any way you can get ahead, you take advantage of it.

"You have to have the right situation to do it. If you feel it's your best chance to score that run whether you're not comfortable with the hitter hitting a sac fly or where the infield is [playing] with the runner on third [you do it]. Whatever the elements might be dictates that you say, 'My best way to score right here is the squeeze.' The only thing you worry about is if they're going to pitch out because they know it's your best chance, too."

Many managers feel that nowadays even relatively light hitters have bulked up so there's a better chance a player can at least hoist the ball deep enough to the outfield to score a run on a sacrifice fly than lay down a decent bunt. Remember, if a batter, even one who's a superb bunter, gets a poor pitch to handle, the runner barreling down from third is trapped in no man's land for an easy out. The offense worked hard to get the man to third, so why take a gamble that could erase him from the base paths?

10. 3 and 5. Bobby Cox believes "Gene Mauch and Sparky Anderson gave a lot of thought into strategy and things like that. I can just tell you I learned a lot from just watching those guys do little things. Those guys originated all that stuff, to me. I thought Roger Craig was pretty much of an innovator himself. Of course, he was with Sparky a long time. Those types of guys would surprise you with stuff; you had to be on your toes."

As for their unusual ploys, Cox said, "I like that type of stuff; why not try it?" He said managers shouldn't merely go by the book and make the obvious managerial moves "when you think something else should work." Plus, he added that trying trick plays is a lot of fun at times.

He even felt "the hidden ball trick is always a good one" and should be attempted once in awhile, labeling former Yankees shortstop Gene Michael "the master at that—he was the best." More recently, Spike Owen and Matt Williams succeeded in duping runners on the ancient play.

11. While Bellhorn can't interfere with the catcher, Bobby Cox explained what Bellhorn should do: "The batter should get as deep in the box as he can to force the catcher back in order to [make it harder for him] to make a tag. I'm sure Mauch's the one who thought of that, him or Sparky."

It helps, too, for the batter to be a righty since he'd be standing on the third base side of the plate, meaning his body would obscure the catcher's vision of the runner bolting down the line.

12. After Clemente had fielded a ball, perhaps on a ball Aaron hit for an apparent double, "Aaron," recalled Walker, " would run into second base like he was going to break his stride [slowing down to settle in at second] and Roberto would start to throw [the ball softly back to the infield]. Then, thinking Aaron wouldn't go, he'd drop his head. Then, boom, Aaron would take off to third base." In effect, Aaron, on offense, had tricked Clemente into relaxing, then took an extra base on him.

Deception is a big part of baseball. Just ask a batter who was geared up for a fastball then whiffed on a pitch delivered at glacier-like speed. As Walker pointed out, Aaron's trick led to a risk-free extra base for the Braves.

13. Every time a defensive player touches the ball, that portion of the play must be accounted for. The ruling is 3 [representing

the first baseman] to 4 [Giles, in this case] and on to 1 [Davis recording the putout]. LaRoche even gets credit for an assist on the play, as does Giles, of course.

14. **ANSWER:** It is not a double play. The run counts.

GAME: Whenever the New York Yankees and Boston Red Sox meet late in the season, something interesting is bound to happen. In 1997, when the Baltimore Orioles had all but won the American League East, the Yankees were pursuing a wild card playoff berth and needed a victory against their biggest rivals. Trailing by one run in the sixth inning, the Yankees had Jorge Posada on second and Derek Jeter on third when Tim Raines came to bat.

Raines hit a foul pop that Boston's John Valentin caught before falling into the photographers' pit. Jeter scored and Posada was apparently thrown out at third base when Valentin flipped the ball to Nomar Garciaparra, who then threw to Jeff Frye, covering third.

The Red Sox left the field thinking the inning was over, but the umpires had ruled the ball dead the moment Valentin fell. Jeter's game-tying run counted, and Posada was able to remain at third base. Wade Boggs then ended the threat against his former team when he also hit a foul pop.

The Yankees went on to win the game, 7–6, when Jeter singled home Paul O'Neill with two outs in the bottom of the ninth. New York eventually won the wild card, but lost in the playoffs to the Cleveland Indians.

CALL: When a fielder falls into a dead ball area after catching the ball, the ball becomes dead. If he does this with runners on base, then each runner is awarded one base. In this case, Jeter was awarded home and Posada was awarded third. If a fielder enters the dugout after making a catch or goes in there and catches a fly ball, then the ball remains alive unless the fielder falls down, in which case the ball is dead and each runner gets one base.

15. **ANSWER:** Foul.

GAME: Batting for the San Francisco Giants in 1999, J.T. Snow hit this towering fly ball. The Atlanta Braves infielders could not agree on who would try to catch it, and they let it fall for an apparent base hit. When it continued its journey out of fair territory and finally met the glove of a fielder, its status became one of a foul ball. Snow soon hit another fly ball, but this one was caught for an out. The Braves won that day, 15–4.

CALL: A ball does not become fair or foul until it stops, is touched by a person or other object, bounds past first or third base, or crosses into dead ball territory on a fly. The question is not where the ball has been, but where it is the moment it meets one of these four conditions. In our case, the ball was first touched in foul ground. Despite the unusual way it got there, it was a foul ball in exactly the same way as a ball hit straight back to the backstop.

16. **ANSWER:** The ball is dead, and the runners are awarded one base.

GAME: Houston Astro reliever Doug Henry threw this wild pitch during a comfortable 10–4 victory over the Chicago White Sox in 1998. Runner Ray Durham made it home while catcher Brad Ausmus thought about picking the pocket of umpire Gerry Davis. Even though Durham seemed to score easily on his own, the ball was considered out of play and Durham was awarded one base, meaning that his run counted anyway.

CALL: When a ball gets stuck in an umpire's uniform, it is no different from a situation where the ball rolls into the dugout. It is out of play. On a thrown ball, runners are awarded two bases from the time of the throw. On a batted ball, it would be like a ground rule double (assuming that it was not umpire interference, which is what happens when the umpire prevents an infielder from making a play). In this case, however, it was a pitched ball. When pitched balls go out of play, the award is one base from the time of the pitch.

17. **ANSWER:** One base.

   GAME: The host Cincinnati Reds were trying to break a 2–2 tie against the Houston Astros in 2001, when Pokey Reese singled to start the eighth inning. Pitcher Octavio Dotel's attempt to keep Reese close to first base backfired when his pickoff throw got past Jeff Bagwell. The ball rolled out of play, and Reese was awarded second base.

   CALL: On a pick-off attempt gone astray, the base award depends on the position of the pitcher's foot. If the pitcher throws while in contact with the rubber, then all runners are awarded one base. If the pitcher first steps off the rubber and then throws the ball, his overthrow would be treated the same as an overthrow by any other player and the award is two bases. This is not an arbitrary distinction, because the pitcher's position gives him different obligations.

18. **ANSWER:** The batter is out, and the runner does not have to return to first base.

   GAME: In 2005, the soon-to-be-crowned world champion Chicago White Sox were visiting the Toronto Blue Jays. Timo Pérez started the top of the second inning with a base hit off Blue Jay starter Dave Bush. The next batter, Jermaine Dye, had three balls and two strikes on him when Bush delivered the payoff pitch. Dye swung and just nicked the ball, which went directly into the mitt of catcher Gregg Zaun. This foul tip counts exactly the same as any swinging strike. Dye was out and Pérez swiped second base.The next batter, A. J. Pierzynski, popped out to the second baseman, and Pérez was doubled off to end the inning. The White Sox eventually won the game, 5–3.

   CALL: A foul tip, by definition, is caught by the catcher directly after it nicks the bat. It is counted as a strike, and the ball remains alive. If a batter swings and tips the ball foul (and it is not caught), it is a foul ball, not a foul tip. In our example, had there been fewer than two strikes when the foul tip occurred, then Dye would not have struck out. Foul tip. Foul ball. Different things.

19. **ANSWER:** He is out.

    GAME: Self-described "idiot" and speed-demon Johnny Damon of the Boston Red Sox was on the move during this pitch to Trot Nixon by Tanyon Sturtze of the New York Yankees early in the 2005 season. On the walk, Damon had a free pass to second, but when he stepped past the bag, he put himself in jeopardy. Quick-thinking shortstop Derek Jeter took the throw from Jorge Posada and held the tag on Damon, who was called out following some discussion between the umpires and both managers. Jeter had also tagged out Luis Ugeto of the Seattle Mariners on a similar play in 2002.

    CALL: On a walk, the ball remains in play. If other runners are forced to advance, then they are allowed to walk to the next base. Any step beyond that base, however, and they are liable to be put out if tagged.

20. **ANSWER:** The runner from first is out. It counts as a two-run home run.

    GAME: Late in the 1998 season, Kevin Young of the Cincinnati Reds hit an apparent three-run home run off Pete Harnisch of the Pittsburgh Pirates. But when Jose Guillen ran past teammate Adrian Brown between second and third, he was called out for passing a leading runner. The home run stood, but only two runs counted.

    In recent years, a number of runners have made this basic blunder and belong in a special hall of shame: Brady Anderson, Billy Ashley, Tony Fernandez, Cecil Fielder, Tom Lampkin, Miguel Ojeda, Terry Pendleton, Roberto Petagine, Alex Rodriguez, Ruben Sierra, Michael Tucker, Devon White, Lou Whittaker, and Eric Young.

    A special mention goes to Terry Pendleton of the Atlanta Braves, who passed Deion Sanders during the 1992 World Series against the Toronto Blue Jays and almost caused a triple play. David Justice had hit a long fly ball to Devon White for the first out. Running from first base, Pendleton passed Sanders between second and third for the second out. And then Sanders was almost tagged out on appeal as he ran back to second.

CALL: In most of the cases where a runner is called out for passing his teammate, there is some confusion over whether a fly ball will be caught. One runner is retreating to his base for safety, while a following runner steams ahead and passes him. It is always the following runner who is out in these situations.

21. **ANSWER:** If time is not called, runners can advance at their own risk.

GAME: Pitcher David Cone, playing for the New York Mets in 1990, was sure that he had stepped on first base to record the third out of a half-inning against the host Atlanta Braves. While he was pleading his case to umpire Charlie Williams, Atlanta runners Dale Murphy and Ernie Whitt took the opportunity to sneak around the basepaths. By the time Cone realized what was happening, both runners had scored. The Braves held on to win, 7–4.

CALL: Many players assume that time is out automatically when they argue an umpire's decision. Time is never out automatically, except in special cases like foul balls or a hit batsman. Unless there is a play such as a balk or interference play where a time-out should be called, a player or manager needs to request a halt in the action. Then, umpires must decide whether a play is over. If the play is over, they can call a timeout or not, at their discretion. Once time is out, play does not restart until the pitcher steps on the rubber with the ball.

22. **ANSWER:** No.

GAME: In 2000, Benny Agbayani of the New York Mets joined a long tradition of ball players who have had trouble counting to three. Met pitcher Mike Hampton was trying to protect a 1–0 lead in the fourth inning against the visiting San Francisco Giants, when Agbayani gave the ball to a kid named Jake Burns. On Bobby Estalella's fly ball, San Francisco runners Jeff Kent and

Ellis Burks both scored to take the lead and J.T. Snow went from first to third. Hampton then struck out pitcher Shawn Estes, stranding Snow at third base. Fortunately for Agbayani, the Mets came back to win, 3–2.Before Agbayani's miscue, Larry Walker of the Montreal Expos was the Major Leaguer best known for handing a live ball to a fan. In 1994, Walker snagged a foul pop by Mike Piazza of the host Los Angeles Dodgers and handed it to a kid named Sebastian Nappier. By the time he realized his error and grabbed the ball back, Dodger runner Jose Offerman had gone from first to third. This did not make a significant difference to the game, which ended Dodgers 7, Expos 1.

In 2003, outfielder Trot Nixon of the Boston Red Sox became part of this trio of lameness when he also thought he had caught the third out of a half-inning and tossed the ball into the stands with two Anaheim Angels runners on base. This happened in the top of the ninth inning of a 3–2 game. On the play, Bengie Molina scored from second base to make the score 4–2, and Jeff DaVanon moved from first to third. Two more Angels soon scored, and the game finished 6–2.

CALL: In these cases, handing the ball to a spectator is ruled exactly the same way as any overthrow. All runners are awarded two bases from the time of the throw (or hand-off). The ball is immediately dead.

23. **ANSWER:** The pitcher has to bat and will take the place in the batting order of the player who has left the game.

    GAME: Manager Kevin Kennedy was never very clear about who should be pitching and who should be batting. In 1993, when he was with the Texas Rangers, he sent slugger Jose Canseco in to pitch, with disastrous consequences. In 1996, after both he and Canseco had moved to the Boston Red Sox, he moved Canseco from the DH spot into left field. As a result, pitcher Roger Clemens had a rare American League at-bat. This strange series of events happened in the eighth inning of a game in which the Red Sox had a commanding lead over the Seattle Mariners. You have to wonder—if it was a commanding lead, then why was it necessary to put Canseco into left field for defensive purposes? Was it worth risking injury to the great Roger Clemens, or was this merely a publicity stunt? The "Rocket" had the last laugh that day, when he connected with a 0–2 pitch from Norm Charlton for a base hit. Clemens went on to pitch a scoreless ninth inning to preserve an 11–4 complete game victory.

CALL: The designated hitter rule was introduced into the American League in 1973 for the simple and obvious reason that in the modern game, pitchers (despite Clemens' perfect batting record in 1996) are generally lousy hitters. The rule therefore allows for the offense to designate a hitter to bat in place of the pitcher. The DH cannot bat for any other defensive player.

Things can get a little confusing when substitutions are made. A pinch hitter can substitute for a DH and become the new DH. But if a DH comes in to play defense, then effectively the DH is lost. The pitcher would then take the place in the batting order of the player who leaves the game. This tactic is rarely used, but sometimes it does make sense, for example in an extra-inning game, when there are a lot of pinch hitters, by which point the pitchers tend not to stay in the game very long anyway and so may not come up to bat, and a manager may need to use the DH's particular defensive skills (especially if he is a catcher).

24. **ANSWER:** The runner from first is awarded two bases. It is an improper appeal, and the run counts.

GAME: This play changed the outcome of a game and almost signaled the end of a pitcher's career. The pitcher was former National League Rookie of the Year Steve Howe, appearing in relief for the New York Yankees against the Milwaukee Brewers in 1992. The visiting Brewers were mounting a comeback after trailing by six runs, and this play helped to turn the game around.

On the fly ball to Roberto Kelly in center field, Dante Bichette was the runner who left early from third. When Howe then threw the ball into the stands, runner Dave Nilsson was awarded two bases, moving him from first to third. On the second attempt at an appeal, umpire Rich Garcia ruled that it was an improper appeal, meaning that Bichette's run counted despite the fact that he had clearly left his base before the catch.

This made the score Yankees 9, Brewers 7, with only one out and a runner on third. Had Howe successfully made his first throw to third baseman Charlie Hayes—or if he had simply walked over to third base with the ball—Bichette would have been called out on appeal for leaving the base early, and the score would have been 9–6, with two outs and a runner on first. Eventually, the Brewers completed their comeback and won the game in 14 innings, 10–9. Bichette's run made the difference by helping to force the game into extra innings.

Two weeks after this game, Howe, who had already been suspended from baseball six times for drug-related offenses, admitted that again he had tried to buy cocaine. A month after the incident, he was banned permanently from baseball. That November, an arbitrator ruled that Howe's cocaine abuse stemmed from his attention deficit disorder and reinstated him. Howe went on to play for the Yankees for four more years, but was released in June 1996, just missing the start of the Yankees' run of World Series victories. Within days of his release from the team, Howe was arrested at the airport because he had a loaded gun in his suitcase. Tragically, Howe's troubled life came to a premature end in a car accident.

CALL: Steve Howe was an exceptionally talented player with a very serious problem. Some say that he had the potential to be one of the great relief pitchers in baseball. This is a sad story with clear lessons about the dangers of illegal drugs. In this case, the pitcher's failure to make an unhurried throw to third base from about 50 feet away may have revealed underlying difficulties in his personal life, or perhaps it was just one of those unlucky plays. What the incident certainly shows is that there are widespread misconceptions about what is required to make a successful appeal, and the Yankees made the play harder than it needed to be.

In this play, there were two unusual rules, starting with the overthrow. When a player throws the ball out of play, all base runners are awarded two additional bases from their position at the time of the throw. The main exception to this is when an infielder throws the ball out of play just after a batter makes contact, in which case the two-base award is measured from the time of the pitch.

In the Steve Howe example, there was no pitch—no chance for the batter to put the ball in play—and the two bases were awarded from the time Howe threw the ball over Hayes' head. Nilsson was able to advance all the way to third, even though he was standing on first base at the time of the play. There is another exception to the two-base rule. The other unusual rule in our example is the improper appeal. The idea behind an appeal play is that the defense must earn every out. When a runner leaves his base early, the umpire will act as if nothing has happened unless the defense attempts to make a play.

After making the catch, Roberto Kelly could have thrown the ball directly to Charlie Hayes for the appeal at third. Instead, the Yankees unnecessarily called for a timeout and then had to begin live play again by giving the ball to the pitcher, who then had to stand on the rubber to end the timeout. Once Howe had the ball and had stepped off the mound, he could have walked to third base. Instead, he chose to throw the ball.

The defense only gets one chance to appeal a particular play. If the team commits an error, as Steve Howe did, the out is no longer deserved, and play proceeds as if the infraction never occurred. This is why on Howe's second attempt to appeal third, the umpire signaled neither out nor safe—he no longer recognized the appeal. It was as if Dante Bichette had left after the catch, and his run counted.

25. ANSWER: Yes.

GAME: The Yankees were playing the Brewers again at Yankee Stadium, only this time the roles were reversed. In July 1989, the Yankees were batting, trying to add to their 4–1 lead. Batter Wayne Tolleson offered the bunt, with runners Bob Geren (from first) and Mike Pagliarulo (from third) moving on the pitch. Pitcher Jay Aldrich made the catch just as the ball was about to hit the ground and then threw to first baseman Greg Brock for the third out. This third out was an appeal play because Geren had left early. Pagliarulo had also left early, but because no one appealed third base, the play proceeded as if he had tagged up.Once the Brewers left the field, plate umpire Larry Barnett ruled that Pagliarulo's run counted. The play was so unusual that the official scorer didn't believe it. For the rest of the game, the scoreboard showed the score as 4–1, when in fact it was 5–1. This had no bearing on the outcome of the game except that relief pitcher Lee Guetterman did not earn a save, because Pagliarulo's run meant that the Yankees' lead was greater than three runs. After the game, Yankee manager Dallas Green said he had never seen anything like it before.

These so-called "phantom runs" are very rare. The first recorded instance of one was in 1957 in the old Pacific Coast League. At the time, the PCL was "open classification," which meant that it acted as a sort of third Major League. In a similar situation, umpire Al Somers declared that a run had scored even though the runner from third had failed to tag up. Manager Joe "Flash" Gordon of the San Francisco Seals protested the game. Somers had a reputation as one of the game's most knowledgeable umpires, and the rulebook was soon changed to account for his interpretation of the play. "They thought I was crazy," Somers said. "I'll tell you one thing—I didn't think I would be able to get out of the stadium that night."

During the same season, there were two other "phantom runs," one in the International League in a game between the Buffalo Bisons and Toronto Maple Leafs, and one in the American

League that involved the Boston Red Sox and Cleveland Indians. With Boston runners on first and second with one out, Cleveland shortstop Chico Carrasquel made a diving catch in short left field. By the time he completed a double play with a throw to first base, runner Gene Mauch had scored all the way from second. Umpire Hank Soar later awarded the run, which made the score Boston 11, Cleveland 0.Cal Hubbard, the American League umpire supervisor, later explained, "If they know the rules, they'll know what to do. If not, it's their tough luck." This was a little disingenuous because the rulebook was not changed to account for this situation until the following year. But today's players have no excuse!

CALL: The most confusing aspect to the "phantom run" stems from the common misconception that no run can score on a play where the third out is made. It is true that in many cases no run can score on a play that ends a half-inning. There are two basic types of half-inning-ending plays: (1) plays where the batter makes the third out before reaching first base, and (2) plays where the batter either reaches first base or, if he fails to reach first base, plays where he does not make the third out himself. On the first type of play, no run can score no matter what else happens. The second type of play is a timing play, and runs can score if they occur before the third out. The one exception to this simple rule is a force play. When the third out is a force out, then no run can score because a force out is considered to be, in effect, the same as the batter not reaching first base.

In the first example above, batter Wayne Tolleson made the second out, not the third out. Once the batter was out, the force situation was removed, and Bob Geren retained his right to first base. At this point, it became a timing play. The question was whether the third out would be recorded before the run scored.

Once the Brewers made the third out, they were in a difficult situation. The rule book states that a half-inning has only three outs. As it happened, Milwaukee ignored the runner from third.

But what if they wanted to appeal third base after the third out? Would Pagliarulo's run still count?

The rulebook has an answer for this, and it is called an apparent "fourth out." If the Brewers had been more aware of the situation, then after the play they could have taken the ball to third base, recording an out on Pagliarulo on appeal, which would replace the out on Geren in the official scoring. It would look like the Brewers made four outs in the inning, when in reality they would still have just made three, since Geren's out would be withdrawn. It would not count as a triple play. This is the fairest way to protect the defense from having a run scored against them that is not deserved. But they must pay attention and make the appeal. Officially, the defense can make an apparent "fourth out" at any time until the pitcher and all the infielders have left fair territory on their way back to the dugout.

This is all theory. In practice, the play is very rare. I am not aware of an apparent "fourth out" ever actually being recorded in the Major Leagues. But stay tuned, and you may just see one!

26. **ANSWER:** On a dead ball, a runner can return to tag up, as long as he has not already advanced to the next base. Despite being awarded additional bases and despite the overthrow, he does need to tag up or he is at risk of being called out on appeal. On an overthrow, he is awarded two bases from his last legally acquired base, which in this case means he gets second and third.

GAME: It is amazing how many Major League baseball players do not understand that they must touch all of the bases in order. Perhaps Melvin Mora of the Baltimore Orioles was still rusty from the off-season when he forgot this basic baseball principle on opening day in 2001. Trailing the visiting Boston Red Sox, 1–0, the Orioles were rallying in the fifth inning. With Mora leading off first base, Brook Fordyce lined out to third baseman Shea Hillenbrand, who threw the ball into the crowd in an attempt at a double play. The umpires awarded Mora third base, which he took without bothering to go to second. When Red Sox ace

Pedro Martinez put the ball back in play, he made a successful appeal at second, ending the threat and the half-inning.

The Orioles scored in the next inning, thanks to an RBI single by Mike Bordick, and then went on to win in 11 innings, 2–1. It's too bad that Bordick had not paid better attention to his teammate's baserunning miscue, because he made a similar mistake two years later.

In 2003, playing for the Toronto Blue Jays, Bordick found himself in Mora's position in a game against the host Texas Rangers. Bordick was running from first base when Vernon Wells hit a line drive. The ball deflected off Ranger pitcher Colby Lewis and straight into the glove of third baseman Hank Blalock for an out. By this point, Bordick was rounding second. Blalock then fired the ball into the crowd behind first base. On the overthrow, Bordick continued on to third base without retagging first.

After Texas manager Buck Showalter checked that Lewis was not injured, Lewis put the ball in play and retired Bordick, on appeal, at second base, ending the half inning. The Rangers went on to win, 5–4.

CALL: Even when a runner is awarded bases on an overthrow, he must still tag up and touch all the bases in order, or else he puts himself at risk of being called out on appeal. Both Mora and Bordick needed to retouch first base after the ball had gone out of play, and then proceed to second before finally advancing to third. Neither of them did this, but they each took different routes to third base.

Mora failed to touch both first and second base and simply proceeded to third on the overthrow by cutting across the diamond. He could have been called out on appeal at either base (or by being tagged). Bordick's miscue is a little more complicated. Because he had already passed second base, he would have had to retouch second, then retouch first, then step on second base a third time before proceeding to third base. According to the rules, however, when the ball is dead (as in the overthrow), a runner cannot go back and retouch a base after he has already reached the next base. Bordick's only chance of retouching first would be if he had already returned to second base by the time the ball went out of play.

In Bordick's case, the Rangers really should have made the appeal at first base. Instead, they appealed at second, which Bordick had actually touched after he failed to tag up at first base. It seems that the umpires reasoned that Bordick's failure to retouch second base (as would have been required had he gone back to retouch first base) was enough to warrant calling him out at that base as well. The rulebook does not actually discuss this situation. But common sense tells us that the Rangers made a good appeal and that Bordick had run the bases incorrectly, so he deserved to be called out.

These overthrows do not nullify the defense's ability to appeal, despite the fact that teams only have one chance to appeal a particular play, because in a sense the runners committed an additional violation when they failed to retouch a base during the dead ball.

27. **ANSWER:** The play stands because there was no appeal.

GAME: Baltimore Orioles batter Jay Gibbons was in the fourth slot in the batting order and Tony Batista was in the fifth slot during a game against the visiting New York Yankees in 2003. But in the first inning, Batista jumped in front of Gibbons and got an RBI in this batting out-of-turn situation. Yankee manager Joe Torre did not notice and did not appeal, so the umpires let play proceed without reference to the miscue. Had Torre appealed, Gibbons would have been called out, the runners would have returned to second and third, and Batista would have been due up again.

The moment the next pitch came in to Gibbons, however, Batista's at-bat became legal. This meant that the run stood and the next proper batter due up was the person in the sixth slot in the lineup, Brook Fordyce. Gibbons, also batting out of turn, was retired to end the inning. But, by the time the Orioles batted again, Gibbons's at-bat had become legal, so the next batter should have been the person who followed him in the order—Tony Batista! Instead, Fordyce batted and made an out. For the rest of the game, Baltimore went back to the correct batting order.

Baltimore's first-inning run made a big difference in this crazy game, which featured a blown save in the ninth inning by the Yankees' Mariano Rivera, a 12th-inning home run by teammate Jason Giambi, and one of the weirdest plays ever to end a game.

In the bottom of the 12th, with the Yankees now leading 5–4, the Orioles had Jack Cust on first base with two outs when Larry Bigbie hit the ball deep to right field. Cust ran all the way past third base and got caught in a rundown. The Yankees misplayed the situation, however, and let Cust sneak past catcher Jorge Posada with no one defending home plate. With a mere 25 feet to go to score the tying run and no one standing in his way, Cust fell down, and was tagged out by Aaron Boone.

In this play, Cust's slip-up lost the game for the Orioles and drew attention away from the embarrassing fact that Torre's failure to appeal was the reason the game was in extra innings in the first place. This was a rare mistake by Torre, who had a history of understanding batting-out-of-order situations. In a game in 1996, Torre's appeal nullified a single by Matt Mieske of the Milwaukee Brewers, who had batted in place of Jose Valentin. Valentin was called out, bringing up Mieske again, who hit a pop fly. Despite the setback, the Brewers won that day, 4–1.

28. **ANSWER:** The double is nullified and the pitcher is called out.
   GAME: Early in 2004, Cubs manager Dusty Baker was guilty of not informing the umpires of this "double-switch," where an additional lineup change is made while replacing the pitcher in order to move the pitcher's place further down in the batting order. With Cincinnati Reds manager Dave Miley already ejected from the game after he had argued a called strike, substitute manager Jerry Narron alerted the umpires to the out-of-order situation.

   Ramon Martinez was the unlucky shortstop whose double was erased from the books after the appeal. Pitcher Kent Mercker was called out for failing to bat in the correct spot. Dusty Baker did not take this well. He argued with the umpires, threw his hat twice, threw his copy of the lineup card, kicked a bat, and got ejected from the game. Despite having the double nullified, the Cubs won in dramatic fashion in the bottom of the ninth when Sammy Sosa and Moises Alou hit home runs on consecutive pitches to make the score Cubs 11, Reds 10.

This was not Baker's first experience of batting out of order. In 1980, as a player, he batted in place of Los Angeles Dodger teammate Ron Cey, who was actually due to bat. After Baker grounded out, Cey was called out following an appeal by Philadelphia Phillies manager Dallas Green, and Baker's at-bat was nullified. This brought up the batter who followed Cey in the order—Dusty Baker. Given a second chance, Baker hit a three-run home run which proved decisive in a 12–10 victory.

CALL: Batting out of turn can seem confusing to managers, players, and fans. But the rule is actually very simple if you remember these easy guidelines:

Batting out of order is an appeal play, so the game continues as normal until the defense notifies the umpires of the infraction.

If the appeal occurs after the improper batter completes an at-bat, the play is nullified (although stolen bases, balks, etc., still count), the proper batter is called out, and the next batter is the one that follows the proper batter in the order.

If the appeal comes before the at-bat is over, then there is no out recorded and the proper batter comes in to bat, inheriting the ball/strike count that the improper batter had.

In the absence of an appeal after an improper batter completes an at-bat, if a pitch is then thrown to the next batter or if there is some other play, then the improper batter becomes, retroactively, the proper batter. This is the tricky part of the rule, but it makes sense if you remember that without an appeal, the game proceeds as if there had been no infraction. It explains why, in the Yankees–Orioles game, Tony Batista was not the only person who batted out of order. Gibbons was also out of order when he followed Batista, and Fordyce was out of order when he followed Gibbons.

In theory, it is possible that through some arcane process of players batting out of order that the next proper batter would already be on base. In this unlikely case, the player's spot in the order can be skipped.

29. **ANSWER:** It is a forfeit, and the official score is visitors 9, hosts 0.
GAME: In 1979, the Chicago White Sox hosted the Detroit Tigers for a twin bill. The Tigers won the first game, 4–1. Then Comiskey Park became a war zone. It was Disco Demolition Night, a promotion where fans received a discount if they brought along a disco record to burn between games. When the records went up in smoke, thousands of frenzied disco-haters rushed onto the field. There was a fire in the outfield, destruction of the pitcher's mound, and damage to some of the fences. Detroit earned a 9–0 forfeit victory and a sweep of the doubleheader.

This was not the first or the last misguided baseball promotion that cost the home team the game. In 1974, the Cleveland Indians, hosting the Texas Rangers, staged a dramatic comeback to tie a game at 5–5 with two outs in the bottom of the ninth. With Cleveland on the verge of a miracle victory, hundreds of drunken fans attacked right fielder Jeff Burroughs, and both teams' benches emptied as the players went to rescue him. It was 10-Cent Beer Night in Cleveland, and the 23,134 fans at the stadium were making the most of it. Earlier, in the seventh inning, Texas manager Billy Martin had been forced to evacuate his bullpen, which was close to the rowdiest spectators. During the ninth-inning brawl, umpire Nestor Chylak and Cleveland pitcher Tom Hilgendorf were both hit on the head. The game was forfeited to the Rangers.

A more recent incident occurred in 1995, when the Los Angeles Dodgers gave out promotional baseballs to their fans during a game against the St. Louis Cardinals. Dodger batter Raul Mondesi struck out on a controversial pitch in the bottom of the ninth, with St. Louis leading, 2–1. Both Mondesi and manager Tommy Lasorda were ejected, prompting the fans to throw their baseballs onto the field in protest. After a delay in which the players fled the field for shelter, the fans erupted again with a baseball barrage. The umpires awarded the Cardinals a forfeit victory.

CALL: The home team has the responsibility to provide a playable field and safe environment. Any disruption that lasts more than 15 minutes can lead to a forfeit in favor of the visitors. The umpires also have the discretion to terminate a game where they, the players, or the fans may be in danger.

30. **ANSWER:** 3. Eject the batter from the game.

GAME: There were two outs in the bottom of the eighth inning when Pittsburgh Pirate Jack Wilson came to bat against the Arizona Diamondbacks early in the 2003 season. The Pirates were trailing 2–1, giving added importance to every base runner. Diamondback shortstop Tony Womack, moving to his left, fielded Wilson's grounder and fired to first for an unlikely out. The instant replay, however, seemed to show that Wilson was safe. When he raised this point with umpire Fieldin Culbreth, all he achieved was an early shower. The inning was over, and Arizona held on to win, handing Pittsburgh its eighth loss in nine games.

CALL: There is no instant replay in baseball. There are many reasons for this, both practical and philosophical. Purists believe that it is preferable to live with the odd umpire error in judgment rather than sit through countless delays and arguments as fractions of a second are debated over different angles of television footage. It is certainly much more dramatic for fans to witness decisions being made on the field. Plays in baseball are never nullified retrospectively with a yellow flag, as in football, and fans never have to wait patiently for decisions to appear on the scoreboard. While teams are entitled to file protests over umpires' rules interpretations, there is no higher authority when it comes to judgment calls. In this example, Wilson appealed what he thought was a higher power—television—thereby questioning not only the judgment of the umpire but his authority to make the correct decision. The result was an ejection.

31. **ANSWER:** The batter is awarded first base. In cases of a hit batsman, the ejection of the pitcher is only automatic if the umpire believes that he acted intentionally. If a warning has been issued and the act is intentional, then the manager is automatically ejected as well.

GAME: The Minnesota Twins were visiting the Oakland A's early in the 2003 season. Just a few months earlier, the Twins had beaten the A's in a tightly contested five-game divisional playoff series. In the fifth inning on this particular day, Minnesota pitcher Rick Reed plunked Oakland's Ramon Hernandez. Just one inning later, trying to protect a one-run lead, Oakland's Tim Hudson hit Minnesota's Bobby Kielty. Both benches emptied during these two incidents. The umpires did not believe that Hudson hit Kielty on purpose. The next batter due up was the fence-swinging Torii Hunter, and it seemed unlikely that Hudson would choose to face him with a man on base. The A's went on to win, 4–1.

CALL: There is an old tradition in baseball that says that pitchers must "protect their players" by intentionally throwing at players on the opposing team if they think that one of their own players was hit on purpose. Needless to say, this is extremely dangerous because it leads to more players getting hurt, and umpires must do all they can to stamp out this so-called tradition. A lot of progress has been made, but there are many cases where it is difficult to be sure of a pitcher's intent. In the overwhelming majority of cases of a hit batsman in the Major Leagues, the pitcher did not do it on purpose.

In the Twins–A's game, the umpires judged that Hudson was not trying to pitch at Kielty, and they let Hudson stay in the game. This seemed to be the right decision, and no other batters were hit that day.

When an umpire thinks that a pitcher has thrown at a batter on purpose, he should immediately eject that pitcher from the game. Where there is doubt, and if the umpire suspects that someone may try to take revenge, he can issue a warning. A warning can only be made if it is made simultaneously to the pitchers and managers of both teams.

An example of a warning like this took place in a 2005 contest between the Boston Red Sox and the Tampa Bay Devil Rays. By then, these two teams had a five-year history of throwing pitches at each other, and there had been five hit batsmen during the first two games of a three game series. In the third game, Devil Ray pitcher Lance Carter threw behind Red Sox batter Manny Ramirez. Umpire Ted Barrett responded by issuing a warning.

Then the next batter, David Ortiz, dove for the floor to avoid a pitch aimed at his head. As a result, both Carter and manager Lou Piniella were ejected from the game. In the bottom of the inning, Boston pitcher Bronson Arroyo and manager Terry Francona were also ejected when Arroyo threw intentionally at Tampa's Chris Singleton. Boston won that day, 11–3.

It is unfortunate that the penalty for hitting a batter on purpose—the ejection of pitchers and their managers, and sometimes fines and suspensions on top of that—does not dissuade all players from engaging in this reckless behavior. I bet that awarding batters an automatic home run, rather than just first base, would end the problem overnight!

32. **ANSWER:** No, but he must leave after facing the next batter.

GAME: Late in the 2000 season, the Chicago Cubs were in a serious slump and would eventually run up a total of 97 losses. When they visited the San Francisco Giants in September, their pitching was in near-total collapse. Pitcher Ruben Quevedo started the day poorly, giving up one run in the first inning and three in the second. Cubs pitching coach Oscar Acosta made a visit to the mound after Quevedo walked Jeff Kent with the bases loaded. Before long, Acosta had been ejected.

The Cubs insisted that despite all of this, they wanted Quevedo to stay in the game. Because the umpires cited manager Don Baylor for a second official visit to the mound during the same at-bat, they made Quevedo leave the game, but not before pitching to the next batter, Ellis Burks. Earlier, in the first inning, Burks had drawn a bases-loaded walk to earn an RBI. Here in the second, he did it again. He would do it one more time, in the sixth inning, earning a total of three runs batted in, despite going hitless that day. The Giants eventually prevailed, 13–2.

CALL: Teams are allowed to visit their pitcher on the mound twice during an inning before they are required to bring in a reliever. There is a little-known restriction that limits mound visits to one per batter. A visit to the mound technically begins when a manager or coach crosses the foul lines and ends when he leaves the mound itself. Once leaving the mound, if the manager or coach goes back to talk to the pitcher, it is considered a second official visit.

In these special cases, the pitcher must leave the game, but not before he finishes pitching to the batter who is either about to start or is in the middle of an at-bat. If a manager or coach is warned not to return to the mound for a second, illegal visit, then he will be ejected. In our example, Acosta was responsible for the first visit and Baylor made the second visit, but had not been warned by the umpires. So Baylor was allowed to stay in the game. Acosta and Quevedo, however, had early showers.

33. **ANSWER:** Yes. He incited the crowd and can be ejected from the game.

GAME: This play occurred in 1994, in the seventh inning of the second-longest rain delayed game ever. With many delays and a close score, the tension was high. When Darren Lewis of the visiting Giants hit the ball, umpire Larry Poncino ruled that it bounded past the third base bag in fair territory before going over foul ground. So he judged it a fair ball. Met third baseman Bobby Bonilla tried to show that he thought Poncino was wrong and pointed to a spot on the ground in foul territory where he claimed the ball had bounced. Poncino ejected him for what the rulebook calls inciting the crowd. After the game, Bonilla and Met manager Dallas Green told reporters that they did not understand the cause of the ejection.

CALL: Baseball probably has the strictest rules in American sports for arguing with officials. Players and managers are expected to argue verbally. Any gesture, such as waving the arms, throwing a hat, kicking dirt, or, in this case, physically pointing out a spot on the ground, can lead to immediate ejection. Bonilla could have stayed in the game if he had told Poncino that he thought the ball bounced in foul territory. But when he pointed to the ground, he signaled to the crowd that he thought the umpire was wrong.

In judging fair/foul decisions on bounding balls near first or third base, it does not necessarily matter where the ball bounced. What matters is where the ball was the very moment when it passed the front edge of the base. So, it is conceivable that the ball bounced in foul territory after passing over the third base bag in the air over fair territory, for a fair ball.

Chapter 10
Extra Innings

YOUR LAST CHANCE AT BAT

This chapter is all about facts, stats, and trivia. Answers on page 221.

1. WHO WAS THE FIRST BATTER to hit 10 HR as a catcher in one Major League season?

1. Charlie Bennett
2. Jack Clements
3. Buck Ewing
4. Duke Farrell
5. Gabby Hartnett
6. Pop Snyder

2. WHO WAS THE FIRST MAJOR LEAGUER with 300 career HR as a catcher?

1. Johnny Bench
2. Yogi Berra
3. Bill Dickey
4. Carlton Fisk
5. Gabby Hartnett

3. WHO WAS THE FIRST NATIONAL LEAGUE PLAYER to get the first two hits of his Major league career in the same inning in his debut game?

1. Bobby Bonds
2. Frank Howard
3. Adam LaRoche
4. Pee Wee Reese
5. Wilkin Ruan
6. Hoyt Wilhelm

4. WHO WAS THE FIRST SWITCH-HITTER to win a Major League batting title?

1. Robert Ferguson
2. Lee Magee
3. Pete Rose
4. Tommy Tucker

5. WHO WAS THE FIRST BATTER to strike out 100 times in a Major League season?

1. Gavy Cravath
2. Jim "Pud" Galvin
3. Babe Ruth
4. Will White
5. Sam Wise

6. WHO WAS THE FIRST MAN to play in the World Series in all of his first four Major League seasons?

1. Frank "Home Run" Baker
2. Joe DiMaggio
3. Orlando Hernandez
4. Johnny Kucks
5. Christy Mathewson

7. WHO WAS THE FIRST MAN to lead off a Major League game with a home run and have that be the only run scored in that game?

1. Heinie Groh
2. Harry Hooper
3. Len Koenecke
4. Kaz Matsui
5. Hardy Richardson
6. Pete Rose

8. WHO WAS THE FIRST MAN to get the first two hits of his Major League career in the same inning in his debut game?

1. Billy Clingman
2. Tom Daly
3. Harry Hooper
4. Billy Martin
5. Russ Morman
6. Hoyt Wilhelm

9. WHO IS THE ONLY PLAYER to hit a grand slam in his first Major League at-bat?

1. Bobby Bonds
2. Bill Duggleby
3. Tony Lazzeri
4. Shane Spencer

10. IN WHAT YEAR DID the Seattle Mariners first finish a season with a winning record?

1. 1989   2. 1990   3. 1991   4. 1993   5. 1994   6. 1995

11. WHICH WAS THE FIRST TEAM to hit 5 HR in one inning?

1. San Francisco Giants, 1961
2. Minnesota Twins, 1966
3. New York Giants, 1939
4. New York Yankees, 1927

12. WHICH PITCHER SURRENDERED Roger Maris' first HR in 1961?

1. Frank Baumann
2. Pete Burnside
3. Tom Cheney
4. Paul Foytack
5. Bill Monbouquette
6. Jim Perry

13. WHO WAS THE FIRST PERSON to broadcast a Major League baseball game on the radio?

1. Harold Arlen
2. Tommy Cowan
3. Jack Graney
4. Harry Hartman
5. Sandy Hunt
6. Graham McNamee

14. THE FIRST MAJOR LEAGUE GAME in which both teams had uniform numbers was between the Yankees and Indians in what year?

1. 1927   2. 1929   3. 1930   4. 1931

15. WHO WAS THE FIRST FIELDER to turn an unassisted triple play in the Major Leagues?

1. Neal Ball
2. George H. Burns
3. Ron Hansen
4. Bill Wambsganss

16. DICK RADATZ SET THE SEASON strikeout mark for relievers in 1964 with how many K's?

1. 148   2. 155   3. 167   4. 174   5. 181   6. 189

17. THE BROOKLYN DODGERS' CAREER record for grand slams (13) is held by which slugger?

1. Roy Campanella
2. Babe Herman
3. Gil Hodges
4. Jackie Robinson
5. Duke Snider
6. Zack Wheat

18. LOU GEHRIG SET THE SEASON record for most homers against one team with how many clouts against the Indians in 1936?

1. 9   3. 14
2. 12   4. 16

19. IN 1984, WHICH PADRES PLAYER set a team season record with 70 steals and another by being caught 21 times?

1. Tony Gwynn   3. Bip Roberts
2. Carmelo Martinez   4. Alan Wiggins

20. WHO IS THE ONLY PITCHER to toss a nine-inning no-hitter in his first Major League game?

1. Babe Adams   4. Vida Blue
2. Bo Belinsky   5. Bobo Holloman
3. Ewell Blackwell   6. Bumpus Jones

21. GREG VAUGHN SET A PADRES SINGLE-SEASON record with 50 home runs in 1998. No Padre had previously hit more than 40. Whose record did Vaughn break?

1. Ken Caminiti   5. Fred McGriff
2. Nate Colbert   6. Gene Tenace
3. Steve Garvey   7. Dave Winfield
4. Carmelo Martinez

22. WHO WAS THE FIRST RIGHT-HANDED BATTER to hit 58 home runs in a single season?

1. Jimmie Foxx   3. Mark McGwire
2. Hank Greenberg   4. Hack Wilson

23. HOW MANY TIMES DID BABE RUTH hit 50 or more
home runs in a season?

1. two   2. three   3. four   4. five   5. six   6. seven

24. WHO WAS THE FIRST BATTER to hit four home runs in
a Major League game in consecutive at-bats?

1. Cap Anson   4. Lou Gehrig

2. Ed Delahanty   5. Bobby Lowe

3. Robert Ferguson   6. Pat Seerey

25. WHO WAS THE FIRST TORONTO BLUE JAY to hit 30
home runs in a season?

1. Jesse Barfield   4. Rico Carty

2. George Bell   5. John Mayberry

3. Jose Canseco   6. Fred McGriff

26. WHO WAS THE FIRST PLAYER in League Championship
Series history with six at-bats in a nine-inning game?

1. Tommie Agee   3. Rod Carew

2. Paul Blair   4. Ralph Garr

27. WHO WAS THE FIRST BATTER to have six consecutive
hits in a single League Championship Series (6)?

1. Paul Blair   3. Paul Popovich

2. Paul Molitor   4. Pete Rose

28. WHO WAS THE FIRST NATIONAL LEAGUE PLAYER
to triple in League Championship Series action?

1. Hank Aaron   4. Bud Harrelson

2. Tommie Aaron   5. Art Shamsky

3. Tommie Agee

29. WHO WAS THE FIRST PLAYER to score four runs in a League Championship Series game?

1. Will Clark
2. Steve Garvey
3. Reggie Jackson
4. Jay Johnstone
5. Bob Robertson
6. Brooks Robinson

30. WHO WAS THE FIRST AMERICAN LEAGUE PLAYER to homer in a 1-0 League Championship Series game?

1. Sal Bando
2. Don Buford
3. Tony Fernandez
4. Dan Ford
5. Harmon Killebrew
6. John Lowenstein
7. Mike Pagliarulo

31. WHO WAS THE FIRST PRESIDENT to attend a Major League game during his term of office?

1. Calvin Coolidge
2. Dwight Eisenhower
3. Benjamin Harrison
4. Herbert Hoover
5. Franklin Roosevelt
6. Woodrow Wilson

32. WHO WAS THE FIRST NATIONAL LEAGUE BATTER to reach 12 career extra-base hits in League Championship Series play?

1. Will Clark
2. Steve Garvey
3. Keith Hernandez
4. Javier Lopez
5. Gary Matthews
6. Willie Stargell

33. WHO WAS THE FIRST PLAYER to homer in his first two World Series at-bats?

1. Bernie Carbo
2. Chuck Essegian
3. Andruw Jones
4. Benny Kauff
5. Gene Tenace

34. WHO WAS THE FIRST PLAYER to reach four career triples in World Series play?

1. George J. Burns
2. Tommy Davis
3. Lou Gehrig
4. Billy Johnson
5. Tommy Leach
6. Phil Rizzuto
7. George Rohe
8. Tris Speaker

35. WHO WAS THE FIRST AMERICAN LEAGUE BATTER to come to bat three times in one inning?

1. Ty Cobb
2. Joe DiMaggio
3. Moose Skowron
4. Ted Williams

36. WHO WAS THE FIRST MAJOR LEAGUER to be intentionally walked with the bases loaded?

1. Sam Crawford
2. Jimmie Foxx
3. Napoleon Lajoie
4. Babe Ruth

37. WHO WROTE THE POEM "Casey at the Bat"?

1. Ring Lardner
2. Grantland Rice
3. Red Smith
4. Ernest Thayer
5. Earle Warren
6. Walt Whitman

38. WHO WAS THE FIRST PLAYER to win a Gold Glove in both the American and National Leagues?

1. Tommie Agee
2. Clete Boyer
3. Curt Flood
4. Graig Nettles
5. Bill Skowron
6. Devon White

39. JOHN OLERUD'S .353 BATTING AVERAGE in 1998 set a Mets record. Which Met had previously held the record with a .340 season?

1. Hubie Brooks
2. Buddy Harrelson
3. Keith Hernandez
4. Cleon Jones
5. Dave Magadan
6. Lee Mazzilli

40. WHICH WAS THE FIRST TEAM to have three players with 50 or more stolen bases in the same season?

1. Montreal Expos
2. Oakland A's
3. San Diego Padres
4. St. Louis Cardinals

41. WHO WAS THE FIRST SWITCH-HITTER with 100 hits from each side of the plate in one season?

1. Howard Johnson
2. Pete Rose
3. Garry Templeton
4. Willie Wilson

42. WHO WAS THE FIRST MAN to total three pinch-hit grand slams in his career?

1. Steve Braun
2. Gates Brown
3. Manny Mota
4. Ron Northey
5. Dusty Rhodes
6. Rusty Staub

43. WHO WAS THE FIRST PITCHER to appear in over a thousand games in a career of less than 20 seasons?

1. Dennis Eckersley
2. Rollie Fingers
3. Gene Garber
4. Mike Marshall
5. Lee Smith
6. Kent Tekulve

44. WHO WAS THE FIRST 30-30 PLAYER (30 homers and 30 stolen bases in one season)?

1. Hank Aaron
2. Bobby Bonds
3. Tommy Harper
4. Mickey Mantle
5. Willie Mays
6. Joe Morgan
7. Kenny Williams

45. WHO PITCHED THE FIRST PERFECT GAME in American League history?

1. Jack Chesbro
2. Walter Johnson
3. Addie Joss
4. Cy Young

46. WHO WAS THE FIRST AMERICAN LEAGUER to hit a grand-slam home run?

1. Ty Cobb
2. Marty Kavanagh
3. Napoleon Lajoie
4. Herm McFarland
5. Ray Morehart
6. Kenny Williams

47. WHO WAS THE FIRST MAJOR LEAGUE PLAYER to hit a home run in a night game?

1. Lou Boudreau
2. Dolph Camilli
3. Babe Herman
4. Ducky Medwick
5. Johnny Mize
6. Johnny Pesky

48. WHO WAS THE FIRST MANAGER to be ejected from two games in one day by the umpires?

1. Charlie Comiskey
2. Connie Mack
3. John McGraw
4. Mel Ott
5. Paul Richards
6. Earl Weaver

Chapter 10
ANSWERS

1. 4	**9.** 2	**17.** 3	**25.** 5	**33.** 5	**41.** 3
2. 2	**10.** 3	**18.** 3	**26.** 2	**34.** 5	**42.** 4
3. 3	**11.** 3	**19.** 4	**27.** 2	**35.** 4	**43.** 6
4. 4	**12.** 4	**20.** 6	**28.** 4	**36.** 3	**44.** 7
5. 5	**13.** 1	**21.** 1	**29.** 5	**37.** 4	**45.** 4
6. 2	**14.** 2	**22.** 1	**30.** 1	**38.** 1	**46.** 4
7. 5	**15.** 1	**23.** 3	**31.** 3	**39.** 4	**47.** 3
8. 4	**16.** 5	**24.** 5	**32.** 2	**40.** 2	**48.** 4

INDEX